BUILDING A QUALITY CUSTOM HOME

What You Need To Know

BUILDING A QUALITY CUSTOM HOME

What You Need To Know

Ben A. & Brent L. Johnson

with Dave Konkol

BUILDERS PUBLISHING GROUP, LLC

BUILDING A QUALITY CUSTOM HOME
Copyright © 2009 Builders Publishing Group
Published by Builders Publishing Group, LLC
1000 N. Maitland Avenue, Maitland, FL 32751

General Editor: Todd Chobotar
Copy Editor: Jackie M. Johnson
Production Editors: Katherine Johnson
Project Coordinator: Pam David
Book Design: Chip David, Creative KX-3.com, Adam Meyer, CrystalClearArt.com

This book is a work of advice and opinion. Neither the authors nor the publisher is responsible for actions based on the content of this book. It is not the purpose of this book to include all information about building a house. The book should be used as a general guide and not as a totality of information on the subject. In addition, materials, techniques and codes are continuously changing so please understand what is printed here may not be the most current information available.

This book contains numerous case histories and client stories. In order to preserve the privacy of the people involved, the authors have disguised their names, appearances, and aspects of their personal stories so that they are not identifiable. Stories may also include composite characters.

ISBN-13: 978-0-9799736-8-0

Printed in the United States of America

9 8 7 6 5 4 3 2 1

First Edition

CONTENTS

Part II: During Construction

Part III: Helpful Checklists

DEDICATION

This book is dedicated to our Dad Ken Johnson, who taught us what business is all about and reminds us that the customer is always more important than the project itself.

Ben and Brent Johnson

AN IMPORTANT NOTE FROM THE AUTHORS

Please note: Although there are three co-authors on the book they have chosen to write in the first person singular (I, me, my, etc.), as if only one person were speaking. This makes both the writing and reading much easier. So, although stories, illustrations, or examples may come from either author, they have been written as if coming from "one voice."

Also note: In order to achieve an easy flow of language, this book has been written using the singular pronoun "he" when referring to a builder. The authors realize there are many wonderful builders who are women, but have chosen to avoid the awkward use of "he/she" and have chosen instead to use the traditional masculine pronoun when referring to a builder. No offense is intended in this regard; the decision was made merely to achieve simplicity and flow of language.

BEFORE YOU BEGIN

Over the years, my brother Brent and I have been asked countless questions about the things you need to know before building a custom home. Where do you start in the planning and design process? What should a homeowner's expectations be before, during and after construction? How involved should a homeowner be in the construction process? How truly customized can I make my home? All of these questions and more come up in our meetings with potential clients who are thinking about building their dream home. They realize the importance of and the need to understand the process and the critical ingredients to a successful project. To us, it's a simple and straightforward process because we've been in the custom home design and building business for more than 16 years. I think B&B Builders offers an advantage to our clients because we set out to create a company the way we thought it should be done and how we'd like to be treated if it was our home under construction. Our clients come to us with their dreams and we design a home the way they want, not what we think they should have. Integrity, quality and service are the benchmarks of our company–when we say we're going to do something, we do it-at the price we quote. We are open and straightforward about costs, and if you need to talk to us you will rarely have to wait until even the next day. We also share the belief that it is important to provide, not only a one of a kind home, but a unique and exceptional experience, one that can only be achieved through a process that is designed to be effective and efficient.

If you have never built a custom home, or you are considering building another one, then this book is for you. We've combined our decades of experience and knowledge to write this book to save you time, headache and money. It is equally important to us to help you prevent the heartaches and disappointments that result from a lack of planning and to give you sound advice. Brent and I also decided to write this book because of the satisfaction we get from helping people realize one of life's great accomplishments: planning, designing and building their dream home. Our desire is to share practical information in an easy-to-read format to make you comfortable with the entire home building process.

We first learned about hard work from our father when we were just kids. When I was 12 and Brent was 10 years old, we helped our Dad build the house that he still lives in today. It always made us feel good to hear Mom and Dad tell people that we helped build that home. Dad owned an ornamental iron business and Brent and I worked alongside him to fabricate and install railings, spiral stairways, fireplaces and etc. The work was hard and the days were long, but we learned that keeping track of time or watching the clock wasn't what was important. The important thing was to complete the job that you set out to do. Dad believed in staying on the job until it was done and making sure it was right the first time. We also learned how important it is to treat people the way you would want to be treated. Dad's approach to business is evident in our company today–we give clients the home they want for the price we quote them and remain open and honest through the good news and the bad news as well. Our business philosophy has afforded us many repeat clients and referrals that have helped make B&B Builders one of the top builders in the area.

At B&B Builders we know that every custom home we build teaches us something new. If we find a process that helps make the construction run smoother, then we incorporate it into our workflow. Over the years, we both have gained a lot of wisdom in the school of hard work as well as the school of hard knocks. B&B Builders has consistently received top honors in the *Parade of Homes* and we've earned a stellar reputation among our peers, our trade partners and most of all our customers for our designs and home building process. We always cringe when we hear horror stories from people who rushed into a building project without the benefit of experienced professionals and a realistic plan and strategy. At B&B Builders, our goal *every day* is to first listen, and then coach and lead people through a process that we have fine-tuned over many years to ensure the success of our clients. We want your story to be one that ends well and one you will take great delight in sharing with others.

Home is the place where you gather and spend time with your family and friends, a place that you love to live in and where you create memories that last a lifetime. We want you to experience a sense of accomplishment and satisfaction that comes from creating your own unique home. From our first meeting with clients, we set out to form a realistic budget and construction plan. Throughout the home building process, we schedule regular meetings at the job sites with our clients. To ensure our clients remain in the loop on every detail of the project, we set up an email link on our website. When a homeowner has a question, they can directly contact a project supervisor, architect, designer, Brent or myself. Everyone involved in the project automatically receives a copy by email and any responses. Help is just a click away and we find this form of communication helps keep the building process running smoothly and efficiently.

Your home is much more than a physical structure; it is an extension of who you are. Making the choice to build a quality custom home should be a rewarding and exciting adventure. Without the right guidance and the right team it can become overwhelming and be a frustrating experience filled with problems and delay. Our desire and hope is that this book will be a helpful resource that not only equips you with the tools you need to evaluate and plan well, but also provides you with the confidence and inspiration to build your dream home.

Ben and Brent Johnson

PART I

BEFORE YOU BUILD

Should I Build, or Should I Buy an Existing Home?

"To build or to buy." That's the primary question to answer before building a new custom home. To help you decide, ask yourself these ten important questions. Be very honest. Answer each one carefully. Keep in mind that there are no right or wrong answers. You're simply trying to determine the best course of action at this point in your life.

Questions to consider: (Yes or No)

1. Do I have a hard time making decisions?

2. Once I make decisions, do I struggle with wanting to change them?

3. Am I a perfectionist?

4. Is my schedule so busy it's difficult to find time to do the things I enjoy?

5. Does uncertainty and lack of control add stress to my life?

6. Am I regularly disappointed by interactions with other people?

7. Do I handle conflict by looking for the win/win solution?

8. Do I have some available time in my life for the next two to three years?

9. Am I realistic enough to recognize that things aren't always perfect?

10. Is our family life stable enough to handle the additional activity?

If you answered "no" to the first six questions and "yes" to the last four, you're ready to build! If not, you may want to consider waiting on the building process. If your answers were different on more than three or four questions, I suggest you buy a house that is already built.

In a consumer-driven economy, many families have been stretched and stressed because the timing wasn't right or they weren't the right profile of person to be building a custom home. They would've been better off buying an existing home than going through a process that wasn't suited for their life stage, temperament, or timing.

Let's look at an example of a couple that wasn't ready for the custom homebuilding process: In some ways, Josh and Melinda seemed to be ideal candidates to custom design and build a new home. However, it soon became apparent they had difficulty making decisions (see question #1). In addition, Josh was consumed by the demands of his business since he had just launched his own company three years before (see questions #4 and #8).

Josh and Melinda were habitually late for their appointments. In addition to the pressing demands of business, it turned out they were in the midst of an intensely personal family situation that was consuming their time and attention (see question #10). It became apparent that this lovely couple did not have the time at this point in their lives to spend custom designing and building a home. A quick look at the 10 questions above clearly indicated it wasn't an ideal time for Josh and Melinda to build a new home.

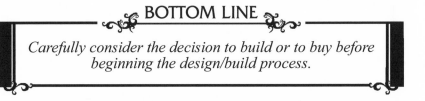

BOTTOM LINE

Carefully consider the decision to build or to buy before beginning the design/build process.

Which Comes First:
The Builder or the Designer?

Just like the proverbial "chicken and egg" question, "Which comes first?" is a question that confuses some people, but must be answered before you start the custom, homebuilding process. While the answer may seem obvious, it's important to know the right answer in order to avoid problems from the beginning. The designer comes before the builder, right?

Wrong! Read on…

Sometimes people get the cart before the horse and in all the excitement, they get ahead of themselves. Mike and Janine thought they had done it all right. They had a roll of plans tucked under their arms, a sparkle in their eyes, and a skip in their steps because they knew they had something very special—they had the plans to their dream home.

During the last several months, Mike and Janine had spent countless hours dreaming about their new home and holding meetings with their designer. They went through revision after revision poring over the plans until late in the evenings. The couple worked tirelessly to make every room just right—put the baby's room here, move the daughter's room there, make that closet just a bit wider, add two feet to the kitchen—giving instruction upon instruction to their designer about each room.

Their dream home included the newest ideas from *This Old House,* the latest trends in low voltage lighting, and cutting-edge insulation that could lower energy bills by up to 90 percent. It had a cabana like the one they saw while vacationing in Acapulco, layers upon layers of moldings, extra tall ceilings, an additional bay in the garage, a steeper roof that was changed—not twice, but three times—because their friends told them it looked too shallow.

Mike and Janine were now ready to find a builder. They were so excited! Janine was bubbling over with her plans—holiday decorations, birthday parties, and dinners with all the aunts, uncles, cousins, and grandma. They had their finished plans and they were now ready to build. They could see it; they could taste it; they could hear the sounds of laughter around the table.

Then the moment of truth arrived.

They were ready to talk to a builder and get him started on their new house. But here was the problem: the actual cost to build this house—the house they had labored over for so many hours, over so many months—ended up costing 75 percent more to build than they expected.

How did this happen? Well—they asked the designer and he gave them his estimate of what it would cost. That's what they based their plans on *The designer's estimate.*

That is the problem. The designer is not trained in doing cost estimates. This news was so devastating to them that Mike and Janine just rolled up their plans, walked out the door, and... sold their lot.

Their dreams had been shattered and they were crushed. After all their initial efforts, they couldn't gather the energy to start the process all over again. It could have been different. If only this enthusiastic couple had known the importance of which comes first: the builder, not the designer.

If you're in this predicament and you're unwilling to sell your lot, turn the page and discover what happens next by reading Jim and Linda's story.

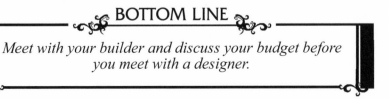

BOTTOM LINE

Meet with your builder and discuss your budget before you meet with a designer.

Forcing a Round Peg into a Square Hole
Finding a Competent Builder

Jim and Linda were the kind of people who refuse to give up. Sometimes persistence is a good thing, but there are times when pushing too hard is unwise. This couple, for instance, were unwilling to listen to sound, professional advice. They forced their opinions and ideas on a builder— and it was like forcing a round peg into a square hole. It just didn't work. Even when they realized they had received inaccurate advice from their designer about their homebuilding costs, they wouldn't give up their dream.

So they began to shop in earnest for a builder who would build their home for the price they were told. Would Jim and Linda find a satisfactory and skilled homebuilder?

Maybe. The builder they seemed to want—one who would be the answer to all their problems—would have been either a builder who was desperate for work or one who didn't know how to price a home.

Finding a competent builder can be challenging, but when you know what to look for, you'll get an accurate estimate and good advice. Many builders won't (or don't know how to) price a home while it's still in the concept stage. If most *builders* can't do this, it certainly makes sense that most *designers* can't either. After all, designers are trained and skilled in *designing* and creating what they are asked to create. Homeowners who don't have a good handle on pricing will tell the designer what they want and the designer will only do what he was retained to do. I'm not blaming designers for not knowing about estimating accurate costs; it's not their area of expertise.

After dozens of exhausting interviews with many builders, Jim and Linda got their homebuilding costs down to a price that was only 20 or 30 percent less than the initial estimate—still well over their budget. They didn't want to give up their dream; they were willing to do anything to bring their dream to fruition.

At this point, Jim and Linda had some choices to make. Instead of cutting their losses and stopping the spending, they continued to pour more and more money into a project that wasn't suitable.

There are plenty of potential homeowners who receive bad advice from a builder and find out one or two years later that their building project is a disaster. Sometimes they begin frantically calling reputable builders in the middle of a project, pleading for help because they finally realize they have relied on poor advice and ended up involved in a lawsuit with their builder.

Please don't do this to yourself. Save yourself and your family the agony of lost time, lost dreams, or lawsuits. Life is too short. It's not worth it.

Get good advice from a competent builder. Interview several first to determine the right one for you and your custom home project. A competent builder will explain the homebuilding process and all the steps along the way. He can guide you through the entire process so you feel confident and secure in your purchase decisions. His firm will have an excellent reputation and be up-to-date on building codes, land, and procedures. Check out the company's references and previous projects completed.

Remember that in building a custom home you are bringing thousands of materials together in an unique way that has never been done before. This process will create some unique challenges for you and your builder. Choose a builder with experience and resources to deal with those challenges.

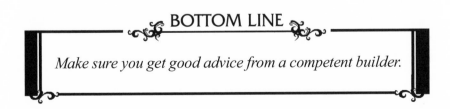

BOTTOM LINE

Make sure you get good advice from a competent builder.

Do I Have to Like My Builder?

So now you've selected a competent builder. But you may ask, "Do I have to like the guy? If he has a good reputation as a builder, does it really matter if I like him?"

Yes, it matters. Don't sign a contract with a builder you don't like, trust, or respect. If you do, you could be headed for trouble.

Why? Because this is a long-term relationship and a long-term relationship with someone you don't like, trust, or respect can be challenging, frustrating, and more than disappointing. The planning stages of custom building a new home can take anywhere from months to years. Actual construction may range from six months to 24 months or longer, depending on the size and scope of your home. Add to that a one- or two-year limited warranty time period, as well as the fact that you may need additional information from your builder for many years to come regarding warranty information, vendor and subcontractor contacts, and other nuances.

In this business, it's not uncommon to lose some contracts to other builders, and it usually boils down to *perceived* costs. A prospective homeowner may initially think our pricing is higher than our competitor, but most often that's because we didn't have the opportunity to thoroughly compare the two proposals.

We like to ask our homeowners why they chose us to build their home. Often the answer is trust. When challenges arise in your project and you call to ask questions, it's important to know that you'll get a straight and honest answer.

Do you respect your builder's values? You don't have to socialize together, but sometimes people choose a builder they actually dislike. Maybe the husband likes the builder or his price, but his wife doesn't care for his style, approach, or manners. Ask yourself this question: Is there a reason you're uncomfortable with this person? If so, why in the world would you trust him to build your single most important investment? If you or your spouse sense that a potential builder operates from a less-than-honest value system, why would you trust him to operate his business with honest values?

During the construction process there will be times when your builder will be making some judgment calls. Many of these will be unknown to you, and that's just part of the business. When it comes to your home, you'll want to know that your builder will be making choices *as if it's his own home*, *as if his own family's safety depended on the choices he makes*. Not just what will pass code inspections. No shortcuts for a quick profit.

Are values important? You bet they are!

BOTTOM LINE

Don't sign a contract with someone you don't like, trust, or respect.

Pick Three Out of Four
Quality, Speed, Service, Price

Jim and Susan had six—count 'em, six—separate flooring companies at their home in a three week period providing estimates to sand and refinish their hardwood floors. About a month later, an unusual sound came from Jim and Susan's house, loud enough that everyone in the neighborhood heard it. There was an explosion of screaming and yelling that continued for several minutes. A hardwood flooring van was parked out front; can you guess what happened? The couple expected a beautiful, high-quality floor, but what they got was what they paid for. They were not happy.

Jim and Susan had selected their hardwood flooring contractor based strictly on price, but somehow they expected they would receive quality, speed, service, *and* the best price. Sure, they probably got the lowest price, but with it came a lot of heartache because they expected more and got a lot less.

It's no different than selecting a builder for your custom home. You need to determine what you value and decide what's most important: quality, speed, service, or price. Of course, you want all four components, but most often you will need to find a builder who can provide three out of four. That's reality.

Is it reasonable to expect that you'll get a builder who will give you the lowest price with great quality, great service, and a timely finish? Let's consider the merits of each:

1. **QUALITY:** A good company prides itself on providing a quality product, especially in the custom home market. They encourage prospective homeowners to look closely at the work they've done for other homeowners and affirm they would be pleased with the excellent workmanship the company provides. Comfort with quality, luxury with outstanding craftsmanship.

2. **SPEED:** An on-time finish is important, but there may be times, especially in a busy market, when a builder misses some deadlines. If that happens, you want your builder to proactively communicate with you and, if possible, find a way to make up the time and get it done quickly.

3. SERVICE: A builder with exceptional customer care will provide good communication and attend to the homeowner's needs before, during, and after their home is completed.

4. PRICE: The best companies aren't usually the cheapest, but consider this: they're probably not the most expensive either. Great companies deliver good value. An honest builder charges at or below market value for the level of service and quality product they provide. Very seldom is the cheapest price the best choice for a homebuilder.

Don't make the mistake of thinking you can have all four qualities in one builder. A Lexus or a Mercedes is priced differently than a Pontiac. If you pay Pontiac pricing (like Jim and Susan) and still expect a Lexus or Mercedes level of performance, you are setting yourself up for disappointment, conflict, and sometimes even a lawsuit.

Know what's important to you and adjust your expectations. If cost is your most important value, then choose the contract with the lowest price. However, if you value quality, be sure you look for excellent workmanship. You can get the results you want in a quality, custom home; just be sure to select your builder based on what you truly value.

BOTTOM LINE

Realistically expect to get three out of four components from your homebuilder. Decide what's important to you.

Where Should I Spend My Money?
If You're Going to Err, Do It Here

Building a home is probably one of the biggest investments you'll ever make, so you'll want to know where to put your money to get the most value for your investment. Here are seven areas to consider:

- **LOCATION:** You've heard the adage "location, location, location." This is where to spend your money. You could build a home with a great design with great features and finishes, but if you build it in the wrong location or on the wrong lot, you could be in real trouble. Consider purchasing the most expensive lot you can afford. Historically, waterfront property experiences stronger growth in value than non-waterfront property. If you like water and can afford it, build on waterfront. Your long-term investment is more likely to be sound.

- **DESIGN SERVICES:** You can add enormous value to your home by investing in the services of a competent designer and an interior design team. Not only will you enjoy the splendor of a fabulous home, you will find a greater return on the money you spend for these services at the time of resale.

- **KITCHEN:** Most buyers don't complain about a kitchen being too large, too much counter space, or too many cabinets. Spend money on the kitchen. We'll talk more about this topic later.

- **FAMILY ROOM:** Oversize, don't undersize, your family room. Families tend to gather and spend most of their time in the family room. If you were to oversize any room, make this room a little larger (rather than smaller) than you think you need.

- **MASTER BATH:** This room is the owner's retreat, a place to relax and unwind. Upgrade your master bath's size and finishes. When you sell your home, this will be an important feature and provide a good investment return.

ROOM SIZE: Make sure your rooms are large enough to meet your needs. It's very expensive to come back after your home is finished and add twelve or eighteen inches to a room because you've just realized it's too small. If you're on a limited budget, it's better to hold off on some of the finishes than cut down the size of your rooms. You can add finishes later, and the cost may only be slightly higher than if you installed them during the initial construction process.

CLOSETS: Never underestimate the value of roomy walk-in closets, linen closets, and laundry rooms.

BOTTOM LINE

Invest your money in the seven places that matter most and you will experience great value for years to come.

What's So Important About the Kitchen Anyway?

W hen a couple buys or builds a home, they always seem to pay a lot of attention to the kitchen. With most couples, there's usually one person who loves to cook; most often it's the woman. For everyone, male or female, young or old, the kitchen is one of the most important rooms in the house. The kitchen is often the hub of the home, the center of activity. Someone spends time preparing food, creating something fun, or trying a new recipe in it. People tend to gather where there's food.

So don't miss this: kitchens are important!

Men sometimes underestimate the importance of this room. We love our garages, grills, decks, and patios. But the kitchen? We can completely miss its importance.

It's important to remember when you are designing a home to consider the resale value and design accordingly. A well-designed and functional kitchen not only makes the cook happy, it also ensures a greater resale value.

A person who loves to cook or create culinary masterpieces for family and friends absolutely needs a spacious and well-appointed kitchen. On the other hand, if a cook wants to spend as little time as possible in the kitchen, then your design and layout can be simpler. Kathy doesn't spend much time in her kitchen, but she likes the spacious layout so she and her husband can be there together. Kathy says the chopping and stirring are more enjoyable with her husband there. Additionally, he likes the organization of a well-planned room.

When selecting kitchen cabinets, look for quality. This is not the place to be overly consumed with trying to save money. Well-made cabinets will provide lasting pleasure and functionality for decades. Drawers (as opposed to cabinets with doors) are more useful and efficient even compared to cabinets with pullout drawers. In addition, choose hard surface, durable, and high quality countertops. There are a variety of colors and selections available. Granite is an ideal counter surface for the most important room in the house.

What about appliances? Don't skimp here, either. You don't have to purchase the absolute top of the line, but good quality appliances help sell homes. Today it's becoming very popular to have two dishwashers. Often the cost of an additional dishwasher is only slightly more than the cost of the additional cabinetry it replaces.

In order to make the most important room in your house spectacular, consider adding some of these other features: warming drawers, double ovens, convection microwaves, pot fillers, espresso and coffee bars, hidden pantries, elevated dishwashers for easy access, vegetable sinks in the island (in addition to the main sink), instant hot water dispensers, and purified water faucets.

When you design your home, be sure the kitchen is given special consideration and that its relationship to other rooms, functions, and features are the best you can provide. It will make a difference for years to come.

BOTTOM LINE

Don't treat your kitchen like any other room in your home. This is one room that deserves special treatment.

Needs Vs. Wants
How to Use the Design Outline to Prioritize Yours

O ne of the best things a homeowner can do is to thoughtfully consider the difference between *needs* and *wants*. It's more difficult than it sounds. For example, something that is considered a *need* to one family member may not be viewed that way by another. Sorting between needs and wants can sometimes be contentious. Take Tim and Sherri for instance. They debated for 45 minutes on whether or not they wanted a formal living room. Sherri, who was raised in a home that frequently entertained guests, considered it a need. Tim, whose idea of entertaining guests was to take them to the game room, did not consider it a need. In fact, Tim felt a formal living room would be largely wasted space.

Discussions like these are far from unusual when building a custom home. They are normal—even essential. I encourage couples and families to have these discussions as soon as possible so that decisions can be made before a lot of design work is done. How can you have those discussions and make them productive and even enjoyable? By using a simple tool called the Design Outline.

The Design Outline is an excellent tool to help you define your needs and wants in the home building process. This exercise takes less than 30 minutes to complete, but it can save you countless hours and thousands of dollars.

Here's how it works:

1. You and your spouse, independently of each other, each take a blank sheet of paper and write down all of your dreams, wants, and needs for your new home, in no particular order.

2. Then rank your items in order of importance, starting with *#1, #2, #3,* etc. It's not as important to agonize over whether item two goes before item three, or three before two; sometimes wants or needs can be equally important to you. What's important here is that *#3 and #28* are not reversed. Know what you want.

3. Once you and your spouse have independently ranked your items, the two of you meet together to share and compare your lists. Then create one combined list ranking your needs and wants in order. This will become your master list.

The combined needs/wants list will save time, energy, and money when you meet with your builder to determine the cost of your new dream home. At some point, your desired budget will need to line up with your desired wants.

Your builder can review this combined list and your budget and let you know what items your budget can afford. If you have items that are not included in the budget, your builder can estimate a cost so you can make an informed decision on whether or not you want to increase your original budget.

The Design Outline can be a tremendously effective tool to help you determine costs long before you spend money on design or construction of your new custom home. You can use the Design Outline with any builder, anywhere in the country. When you begin the process by using the outline, you'll be way ahead of the game.

DESIGN OUTLINE™

Name:			
Address of Property:			
Lot#:	Cost of Lot:	Value of Lot Today:	
Estimated budget for home excluding lot and financing costs:			
Number of Bedrooms:	Number of Bathroms:		
Approx. number of square feet under air:			
Number of Stories: One | Two	Bays in Garage: Two | Three | Four		

COMBINED LIST OF PRIORITIES

1.	11.
2.	12.
3.	13.
4.	14.
5.	15.
6.	16.
7.	17.
8.	18.
9.	19.
10.	20.

⚜ BOTTOM LINE ⚜

Take 30 minutes and complete the Design Outline. It's fun and it can save you countless hours and thousands of dollars.

Should I Use a Fixed-Price or Cost-Plus Contract?
Part 1–Fixed-Price

A fixed-price contract is one in which the plans, specifications, and all of the materials and finishes are fully determined (fixed) before you start construction on your new home. A cost-plus contract takes all the costs of the home and adds either a percentage of costs or a flat fee for the builder's overhead and management fee.

Either a fixed-price or a cost-plus contract can be used successfully in building a custom home. It depends on what you're most comfortable with. The builder's costs are the same whether he uses a fixed-price or cost-plus contract. However, the price you'll pay will differ because of the risk associated with each type of contract.

Let's start by looking at a fixed-price contract.

The advantage of a fixed-price contract is that the price you pay for your home will be predetermined (fixed) whether or not the price of material and labor goes up or down. The builder assumes full responsibility for all risks associated with the cost of your new home. The downside is that you'll pay more for your builder taking on this risk.

On a fixed-price contract, the builder assumes responsibility for all risks associated with the fluctuation in costs. Of course, costs are always changing. From the time you sign your contract to the completion of the work, the actual costs will change. Sometimes up, sometimes down. If labor and material go down from the time you sign the contract until the job is complete, the builder benefits. If the cost of labor and material go up during the construction period, the builder absorbs the loss.

Another factor in pricing a home with a fixed-price contract involves the "fright factor." Will the homeowners change their demeanor once construction begins? No one has ever built a perfect home without some sort of scratch or blemish on it. Any builder can walk into any home in America and find something that's wrong. Anyone can take a magnifying glass and find scratches on any window on any newly built home in America.

Therefore, builders need to charge clients for "fright." If the builder gets to the final walk-through with a homeowner who takes out a magnifying glass and searches every square inch of every window pane in the house, finds a scratch, and wants every scratched window replaced—at the builder's expense—the builder had better have "fright" included in his initial calculations. With a fixed-price contract, the cost of repairing or replacing any and every item that has even a tiny imperfection is all the builder's responsibility.

Generally, people with a fixed-price contract are more inclined to expect imperfect minor items to be replaced because it doesn't cost them extra. To be clear, we're not talking about shoddy workmanship. We're talking about the gray areas of requests that are unreasonable, based on industry standards.

In general, people who do well with a fixed-price contract are people who are not willing to risk price fluctuations. They are more comfortable knowing their exact cost and are willing to pay a small premium for this comfort.

In the next chapter, we will cover the cost-plus contract.

BOTTOM LINE

Choose a fixed-price contract if you are willing to pay a small premium for locking in the total cost of your contract.

Should I Use a Fixed-Price or Cost-Plus Contract?
Part 2–Cost-Plus
—ↄ৵৽–

A cost-plus contract differs from a fixed-price contract in that it takes the actual cost of building the home and adds a fee for the builder's overhead and management. This fee can be either a lump sum (flat fee) or a percentage of total costs. Of course, neither you nor your builder will know the exact bottom line for the building costs until the final accounting is completed shortly after closing. A good builder will give you an accurate cost estimate, but it's exactly that—an estimate—until the final accounting. With a cost-plus contract, you'll pay the actual costs for all labor and material, plus the builder's fee.

A cost-plus contract can be advantageous when building larger, custom homes with finish levels and other things changing during the process. With the cost-plus basis, the homeowners know their actual costs on an ongoing basis. They can then determine where they will appropriate their funds early in the construction process and receive a full accounting disclosure of all costs. If they elect to pull out a magnifying glass to search for scratches in all the panes of glass, they can choose to have those panes of glass replaced at their cost.

Usually, doing business on a cost-plus basis keeps the magnifying glass in the drawer. It doesn't mean the builder builds with less care or quality; it just puts the homeowner and the builder on the same team. A cost-plus contract provides the synergy of identifying problems and determining win/win solutions that are in the best interests of the homeowner.

If you trust that your builder is competent and is working on your behalf, and if you are comfortable not knowing your exact total costs until the end of the project, then a cost-plus contract may be best for you. Your final cost will depend on the choices you make. Your builder will charge a smaller builders fee on a cost-plus basis because he assumes less risk. As part of a cost plus contract your contractor should have a detailed cost estimate before construction begins. As construction progresses you should be given monthly progress reports based on the original estimate, cost to date, estimated costs to finish, any changes to the total cost and the current estimated total cost. This will help to eliminate large surprises in total cost at the end of the project.

Both fixed-price and cost-plus contracts are successfully used in building new custom homes. You can decide which one works best for you.

BOTTOM LINE

Choose a cost-plus contract if you are comfortable knowing your end cost will be determined by the choices you make and you know you have a trustworthy builder.

Don't Even Begin Designing Your Home
Until You've Done This!

There is an ancient proverb that says, "*Suppose one of you wants to build a tower. Will he not first sit down and estimate the cost to see if he has enough money to complete it?*" I suppose it's because I'm a builder, but I can relate to this bit of wisdom. It's a rhetorical question, of course. Who *wouldn't* first estimate the cost?

In reality, it sometimes amazes me to meet with people who are ready to build a new, custom home but have no idea what they want or how much they can spend. Stop right here! It's crucial, before beginning the design/build process, to determine what you can afford.

People who need financing assistance should talk to an experienced professional mortgage lender who can help determine what they can comfortably afford. This process will take into account your income, expenses, credit, assets, interest rate, taxes, insurance, maintenance, and utilities.

Sadly, people who begin the design process without first counting the cost often design to their dreams, only to find out later they have far exceeded what they can afford. They end up mad, sad, or extremely frustrated. Instead, we first want our homeowners to realistically determine what they can afford; then we work hard to design a quality, custom home, a complete package that's 5 to 10 percent below their target number. We know from experience that changes may occur during the building process. For instance, a homeowner may upgrade the finishes as the construction process unfolds, or other variables may arise that would add to the cost of their home. If we start with a number that is below their budget, we can end up at the desired budget.

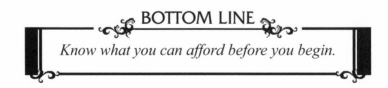

BOTTOM LINE
Know what you can afford before you begin.

Buy a Plan or Custom Design?
Read This before You Decide
—⚭—

Should you buy a ready-made plan for constructing your new home? It depends.

If you have a large lot that doesn't have restrictive setbacks, then finding and buying a ready-made plan may work well for you. It's important to know that most plans you find in a plan book are designed for specific lot sizes and regular shaped lots. If your lot is long and narrow and the plan is designed for a lot that's narrow and long (just the opposite), you could have a problem.

Sometimes people will use the "cut-and-paste" method. A couple will take a plan from a plan book and "cut-and-paste" it to make it fit their lot. Be careful with this method. Judy was a woman whose cut-and-paste plan didn't work out the way she'd planned; it required you to walk through one bedroom to get to another bedroom.

If you can find a plan that fits on your lot with little or no changes, it may be a good option for you. However, very few people are completely happy with a design they find in a plan book without making minor to major modifications.

If you are thinking of buying a ready-made plan and just shrinking it, it almost certainly will *not* work.

Most good, custom-home builders have successfully built homes from ready-made plans. Typically they purchase the rights for the plan, make any needed modifications, and proceed to build the house.

Be aware that ready-made plans are copyrighted. Your builder can purchase the rights for the plan, but be sure this step is not overlooked. You can get in real trouble down the road if you shortcut this step.

For people who don't choose a standard plan, some builders offer a complete design/build package. Usually this process starts by evaluating the shape of the lot; it's important to take into account its positive and negative features. The builder then takes the homeowner's completed list of their prioritized needs and wants and begins the design process. At your initial meeting with the builder, it's an important step to review the design and to ensure the designer and homeowner have a complete and thorough understanding of needs, wants, and budget. Once the builder has clearly identified your objectives, he can work with the designer to create a unique, quality, custom home—the home of your dreams.

As a builder, I've found that it doesn't necessarily cost any more (and often we've discovered cost savings) by first focusing on and designing what our homeowners most *need* while also taking into account what they *want*. In doing so, we've found great success because the process allows us to optimize the conditions of the specific and unique lot instead of having to work from an existing design by enlarging or shrinking areas in the home.

With clear objectives and a good plan, you can focus your energy and resources on your unique needs for your new home.

BOTTOM LINE

If you can find a ready-made plan that requires few or no changes and you just love it, then you may want to consider purchasing a buyer-ready plan. If not, don't make the mistake of cutting and pasting.

Surprises That Could Inflate Your Custom Home Cost

Early in the design process, your builder should work with you to create an estimated line-item budget for your home. Each item (landscaping, appliances, flooring, etc.) should be listed separately with a corresponding dollar amount (allowance). The line-item budget should make sense to you, and the numbers should be in line with the general caliber of work you've seen in other homes this builder has completed.

Several years ago some friends came to us wanting a bid on their house. As always we spent a lot of time asking questions on completing an accurate cost estimate that realistically would finish a home the way our friends wanted it finished. A couple weeks later they informed us they would be going with another builder who had provided a lower bid. We asked them to carefully review both bids and left it at that. Several months later our friends approached us to say, "You were right, we found out the builder with the lower bid had insufficient allowances and did not include some things we had asked for."

Interestingly, an allowance (or budget) can be your friend or it can be your worst enemy. Good, honest, quality builders may lose jobs to the competition because they establish a realistic allowance that truly reflects the scope of the entire job. Conversely, many builders will establish low allowances that are insufficient to build the home with the quality expected. Be wary of a budget that seems too good to be true. You could be talking to an unscrupulous builder who says whatever he has to say to get your business.

Allowances are established by builders because selections are not always made prior to the commencement of building a new home. If a builder provides an estimate for a new home and purposely or unknowingly lists allowances that are not sufficient for the quality expected, the initial bid can be thousands, if not tens of thousands, less than an honest builder's proposal.

The last thing anyone needs is to be in the middle of construction with insufficient allowances to complete the home. A good, quality builder will put a lot of effort into listening to what a homeowner values and then designing a complete home package to meet those needs. He will try to establish budgets (allowances) that allow the homeowners to select items that are in line with the level of quality they want for their home.

One of the biggest challenges for a homeowner and a builder is to identify a sufficient allowance and how all those numbers and allowances play into an overall budget. A major key to a successful project is to take the desired overall budget, consider the needs and wants of the homeowner, and create and execute a home that the homeowner will be happy with for years to come.

After listening to the needs of the homeowners, a builder will establish allowances that are appropriate for that home. After that, you should do some shopping at selected vendors before you sign a contract. This will allow you to get a sense as to whether the allowances are sufficient. If the allowances are not sufficient, you either have to raise the overall budget or reduce allowances or features in other parts of the home. It's important to do this *before* construction begins. If determining allowances happens *after* construction begins, it leaves room for misunderstanding and frustration.

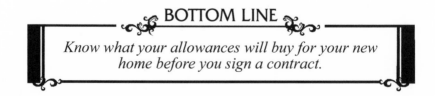

BOTTOM LINE

*Know what your allowances will buy for your new
home before you sign a contract.*

Design Your New Home with Resale in Mind

W ho thinks about resale value when building a home? While it may seem odd for a person who's building a new home to think about selling it, it's important to address what you want and what the market wants even in the initial planning stages. If you're not careful, you may design your dream home and find that no one else will buy it later!

Most people who build custom homes are financially sound. For the most part, they are able to build beautiful, quality homes because they've been making good financial decisions for many years. As you go through your design process, be certain you get wise counsel from your builder, designer, and possibly a real estate salesperson to be sure you're not building a home that only your family will like. Balance your wants and needs for the home of your dreams with potential market appeal for future resale.

You are probably not building your dream home as a spec home (a home without an end buyer before construction begins, generally built with an intended profit), so be careful not to include design features that are not what the broad market is asking for. An experienced builder will guide you through the design process and help protect your investment. Once you have the facts, it's your responsibility to make your own design decisions. If you proceed to design and build a home that only appeals to a very narrow market, then at least you are aware of that (and the consequences) in the early stages of the design process.

Sometimes homes linger on the market for a long time because a homeowner made design decisions without taking into account the long-term resale effects.

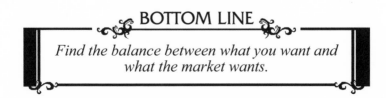

BOTTOM LINE

Find the balance between what you want and what the market wants.

You're Going to Live Here HOW Long?

If you ask someone who is ready to build a new home, they will often tell you that "This is the last home I will ever build. They will have to bury me in the back yard."

Recent surveys show that most people live in their home an average of five years, and you're probably not much different. You may be thinking, *but this really is going to be my last home*. And if it is, that's great. But you may want to consider the reality of averages.

Susan took more than a year to design her new home for her family, only to discover she was way over budget. She also realized that by the time she completed her home construction, all but one of her five children would be away at college, and she had designed bedrooms for each of them! Reality finally dawned on her—within a few short years, she and her husband would be empty-nesters. Designing her home for a family of seven thinking this would be her home for the rest of her life didn't fit the reality of Susan's imminent transition to a home for two.

When designing your custom home, first design for your immediate needs. Second, take into account what market conditions will allow for your particular home design. Third, give strong consideration to how long you may live in your home. Susan may shift gears and design a home that's perfect for her family's needs for the next five to seven years, with a plan to downsize at that time. With this more realistic outlook, she may give additional consideration to the resale value of her choices.

Don't make the mistake of over-designing a home that may become obsolete for your family within a short period of time.

BOTTOM LINE

Be realistic about your short-term and long-term needs and how long you will live in your home, and design accordingly.

Should I Hire an Attorney?

—⁂—

Some people just feel better if their attorney reviews the construction contract, and that's okay. If you do this, be sure you hire someone who knows the real estate and construction business and will complement the process.

Monica loved to stop by and watch the construction going on just a few doors down from her home. She was very observant and noticed the quality of workmanship and materials. Monica not only knew the homeowner, she knew a number of my previous homeowners.

As Monica and I got to know each other, we began planning to build her a custom home. We spent many hours and numerous meetings designing the ideal plan for her lot. Finally, two-and-a-half years later, after three re-dos of her design, we were ready to build.

Three days before the closing date on her loan (signaling the beginning of construction), Monica called me to say her attorney had reviewed my contract and advised that it needed to be completely rewritten. I told Monica I'd been using this contract for many years and had never experienced a request like this. I suggested she ask her attorney for specific comments and told her I was confident we could work through the issues. Monica agreed and said she would get back to me.

The day before the scheduled closing, I received an email from Monica stating that (based on her attorney's advice) she would not be building with me. Obviously, I was surprised.

A few days later, I met with Monica, and she affirmed that she would not be building with me. I told her I was disappointed because we'd been working well together for almost three years. I had counseled her through obstacles, given her professional advice, and taken her through three design changes—all successfully. It was very disconcerting now, after all that, to learn that her attorney was counseling her *not* to proceed without even a willingness to discuss specific points.

Unfortunately, Monica received some bad advice from her attorney. By insisting on an entire rewrite of the contract a few days before closing, he didn't serve his client well.

Monica eventually built her home with another builder. It was close to my neighborhood, so every few months I would drive past the project. A good builder can tell without ever speaking to anyone whether a project is going well or not. By seeing the progress over the months, I observed that the project took six or seven months longer than anticipated. It didn't seem to be a good experience for the builder or for Monica.

I'm not bashing attorneys here; some of my best friends are attorneys. In fact, I have a great attorney, but he provides essential advice that complements who I am and what I do. He helps me design win/win agreements, not win/lose, or lose/lose situations.

If you hire an attorney, be sure to hire someone with construction and real estate experience, not a general practice attorney who counsels on personal business, family trusts, estates, etc.

BOTTOM LINE

Hire an attorney to review your contract if it makes you feel better. Just be certain to hire one who helps you and not hinders you.

How Much Do You Charge
Per Square Foot?

Building a custom home is a bit like buying a new car, right? Not exactly.

If you asked a car dealer how much he charges *per pound*, you'd get some very strange looks. Of course, there is some correlation between the cost of the car and its weight, but not significant enough to prompt that question. We all know car dealers don't sell by the pound.

In the same way, I feel perplexed when someone asks me how much I charge *per square foot* to build a home. It's not the right question.

There are three factors that contribute to the cost of a home, regardless of where it's built: complexity, level of finish, and size and components.

1. **COMPLEXITY:** A home with more features and greater complexity requires more labor, and therefore costs more to build. For example, a rectangular house with four basic corners is less expensive to build than a three-story home with 40 corners, angled walls, and steep roofs, because the latter is more complex and takes more time to complete.

2. **LEVEL OF FINISH:** Obviously, vinyl flooring is much less expensive than wood or stone. Formica countertops are less expensive than granite. Twelve-inch baseboards cost more than six-inch baseboards, and a lot of molding is more expensive than no molding at all. The level of finish you choose for your home will have a significant impact on the home's final cost.

3. **SIZE AND COMPONENTS:** Size matters in homebuilding costs. A 6,000-square-foot home will cost more than a 2,000-square-foot home. A 2,000-square-foot home would probably include a two-car garage, while a 6,000-square-foot home normally has three or four bays. So not only does the larger home cost more due to the size of the heated and air-conditioned space, but it also takes into account things like garages, number and size of porches, whether the home has a pool, boat dock, circular drive, and other costly components.

It's a good idea to ask a builder what price *range* per square foot he builds at, in order to know if you're talking with the right builder.

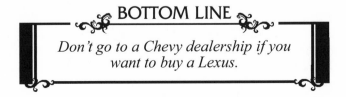

BOTTOM LINE

Don't go to a Chevy dealership if you want to buy a Lexus.

Welcome to Art Class!
Create a Dream Home Notebook
—◦∾◦—

Now you get to have some fun! While you continue to dream about the possibilities for your new, custom home, let's create a "Dream Home Notebook." Gather some magazines and tear out pictures of features you really like or want in your home and, just like you did in art class, start collecting them in a notebook. You may also want to take photos of features in other homes you have walked through. Model homes, friends, or neighbors' homes can be great sources of ideas. Write on each picture specifically what it is you like about it. Why did you tear it out? People often begin collecting pictures but months later they can't recall why they tore it out in the first place. Write it down.

Creating your Dream Home Notebook can be an inspiring and enjoyable activity, and it will be very helpful to your builder and design team. As you accumulate more and more pictures, begin to categorize them. Here are some suggestions for your categories:

1. Exterior features

2. Kitchen features

3. Master bathroom and bedroom

4. Common living spaces

5. Specialty items such as fireplaces, mantles, trim details, paint colors, etc.

6. Colors, textures, styles

7. Any floor plan that interests you. Write down what interests you about a particular plan. It may be the relationship of rooms, the uniqueness of design, or even a small feature like a hidden pantry or a workstation for mom.

8. Things you specifically DON'T like

9. Your written notes

Sometimes it can be difficult to express what you like and don't like in new home features. So the Dream Home Notebook is a helpful resource in the planning process. The saying, *"A picture is worth a thousand words"* also applies to the development of your custom home design. An experienced builder can look at the pictures and listen to the conversation (and often read between the lines) to help you better articulate what you are thinking but are unable to put into words.

It's also helpful to write down your expectations. You may want to include stories (good and bad) of what your friends have gone through in their homebuilding experience. Also write down the elements in your home that are important to you. When you finally meet with your builder, you will have a well-organized, thoughtful notebook to share, which will help tremendously in your design and building process.

There are literally thousands of ways to construct any given item in a home. A good builder will work hard to ensure that the end product turns out as you envisioned it. Your builders understanding of what you want may not always be exactly the same as what you understood. If you have a specific idea of how you would like something done, provide your builder with drawings and information to make sure he completely understand what you want. The more detail you give your builder in a drawing, material, dimensions, etc., the better chance he will have to do it right the first time.

If something turns out different than what you wanted, a good builder will redo the work at your request but reserve the right to charge for the additional work.

BOTTOM LINE

Cut out or take pictures for your dream home and organize them in a single place along with your notes on what you really want.

Close Enough to Perfect?
Identifying Expectations
—❧—

A homebuilder's goal is to create a well-built, attractive home that meets the needs of the homeowners. But how close to perfect does the finished product need to be? What about imperfections or flaws? Brian doesn't care about details, while George is extremely particular and wants every single blemish erased—*every single one.*

What about you? What are your expectations for what you will and will not accept when your home is finally completed? This is definitely something you and your builder need to discuss.

Here's what I often do: I make an appointment to meet the new prospective homeowner at one of our recently completed homes. I have a very defined plan to walk through this new home together and thoroughly inspect all aspects of the home.

I meet the prospective homeowners at the newly-built home and start the inspection in the foyer. As I point out the features, I ask a very specific question. "If we were standing here a year from today and we were doing the final walk-through on *your* new home, would this meet your expectations?" Usually, my wide-eyed prospective homeowners nod affirmatively. Before I move on to the next room, I take a moment and encourage them to look closely at the finish. I tell them that a paint job can never be perfect; I may find a blemish or two on the walls or in the trim work. Then I ask again, "Would a paint job with these imperfections meet your expectations?" Usually, they say yes. Then I ask them to rub their hands over the trim work to feel for smoothness and any imperfections. I'm actually looking for some imperfections in the paint job because I want to clearly identify their expectations.

After we discuss the paint finish, we move on to trim work. From trim work, we move to drywall. From drywall, we move to flooring, and on and on it goes throughout the house. Then we walk into the living room where the same process takes place. I ask the prospective homeowner the same question, "If this was your living room, aside from the paint colors and selections of materials, would this living room and the quality of the workmanship meet your expectations?"

This process is very important. The last thing you or your builder want is to find yourself a year or 18 months into the building of your new custom home, only to discover that each of you had different expectations. I make it a point during the interview process to be sure we have clear expectations of what is or is not acceptable for the quality of the end product—your custom home. By doing so, both parties can avoid unmet expectations, frustration, anger, or even a lawsuit.

BOTTOM LINE

Schedule a one-hour private showing of a home your builder has recently completed. Tell your builder whether the quality meets your expectations or not.

The Terrible Truth about Building
Beyond Your Means

Sometimes homeowners want to build a home that doesn't seem to be affordable for them; it's well beyond their means. That's a tough situation for me because if I build the home the way they want, I know they'll regret it. On the other hand, if I don't, they won't be happy with me. In fact, I've sometimes lost building opportunities simply because I want to be straight with people when it appears they're pushing the envelope of costs.

Of course, I know I'm not my clients' keeper regarding how they spend their money. But as a professional who values integrity, I believe I have a responsibility to share the cold, hard facts of the large investment they will be making in building a home. Some people begin the design process with a realistic budget that's within their means, but as the process moves along, it can begin to get out of hand.

If you've purchased a new car recently, you know what I mean. Say for example, you want to get a nice car and you decide your budget is $30,000. Once on the lot, you see the base price on a model you like is $34,000. *Well, it's only a few thousand more*, you think. But then you start noticing some of the options. You really like the upgraded 10-disc CD changer (only another $1,000), and it's just $19.80 a month more on your monthly payment. Of course, then you see other cool things like the GPS Navigation System, the backup camera, and the Premier Audio System—so you add another $6,000. You also decide to upgrade from the standard leather package to the heated and cooled, comfort leather seats. That adds $2,160, but it's so incredible! Then you discover the Satellite Radio System, and add $486. Finally, you decide to add a sunroof, custom paint, and upgraded tires…

You get the picture.

In a matter of minutes, your $34,000 car became a $45,000 car. And remember, you started out looking for a car that would cost $30,000.

That's what it's like for some homeowners who design and build a home. Construction hasn't even started and already they've added options and selections to their home beyond the original plan. Sometimes people stretch and stretch financially to build their new home and by the time construction begins, they're under so much stress that when we have an opportunity to add a nice feature to their home (something as simple as additional crown molding), they are completely stressed out because of a few hundred dollar decision. That's often because they didn't discipline themselves to stick to a reasonable budget.

Please don't build a dream home you will have to sell before you even move in because you can't afford it.

Be sure you have a builder who will help guide you through this process with honesty and professionalism. If I notice that costs are beginning to exceed the homeowner's budget, I tell them that it's my responsibility to communicate this to them. The final choice is up to the homeowner. Ultimately, I want them to be happy *and* financially healthy with their finished dream home.

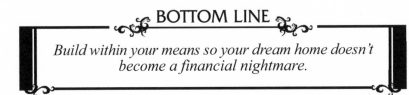

BOTTOM LINE

Build within your means so your dream home doesn't become a financial nightmare.

The Hidden Pot of Gold in Your Pocket

W hen I work with people on a homebuilding project, sometimes couples come to me with a maximum budget for building their new home. They plan a budget for the lot, the home, and architecture—a complete package. When I review it with them, I spend a considerable amount of time listening, asking questions, and working to meet their particular budget. I want to make sure we maximize their investment.

Many times, however, I'd work fervently to create a design, size, and features to meet the homeowners needs and wants within the budget they presented, only to find out later that they had a hidden "pot of gold" in their pocket; they had more to spend than they let on originally.

That approach has always seemed counterproductive to me. After spending countless hours working to meet their budget, and THEN learning the couple actually has an additional amount to spend, we essentially have to go back to the drawing board to start the design process all over again. Not only is it frustrating, it also sets the construction schedule back. So if they thought they'd be in their new home by Thanksgiving, it would now be closer to Valentine's Day. After this hidden amount situation happened to me several times, I started telling my homeowners this true story:

When I first got out of college, I was ready to purchase my first vehicle. I went to the car lot and told the car salesman I wanted to spend no more than $10,000 for a vehicle. He said, "Great. Come out to the lot and I'll show you what I have."

I followed him out, and when he showed me the first car, he said, "Now here's one for $11,500." I looked at him in complete disbelief. I thought, *did you not hear me? My budget is $10,000.* I was thinking he'd start me somewhere in the $8,000 or $8,500 range, so that by the time I paid for tax, title, car handling fee, and other options, I'd end up at my budget of $10,000.

Admittedly, I was young and naïve and didn't know about slick salesmen. I did end up buying a car from him because I didn't know any better, but it gave me a bad taste in my mouth. I told myself then that if I ever had the opportunity to sell someone a product or a service, I'd never sell that way.

I tell homeowners this story because I finally realized they may think I'm like a slick car salesman. So I tell them I treat their money like it's my own. I will honor and take seriously the budget they give me. That's why I need the budget to be accurate, with no mysterious "pot of gold" showing up later.

If you trust your builder, give him your real budget at the beginning of the process. If you don't trust your builder, then you shouldn't be working with him anyway.

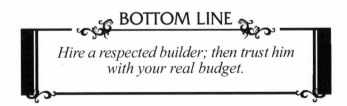

BOTTOM LINE

*Hire a respected builder; then trust him
with your real budget.*

Choices, Choices, Choices!
Choose Before You Lose

I strongly recommend making your selections before construction begins on your new custom home—color, cabinets, plumbing, hardware, paint, and more.

Yes—all selections!

Before I learned how important this was, I noticed that homeowners often seemed unable to make selection decisions in a timely manner. Indecision messes up the deadlines, stalls the project, and can greatly frustrate both builder and homeowner.

Randy is a good example. I gave Randy deadlines for his selections and every single deadline was missed. When it was time to make his paint selection, he asked me, "Well, when do you need it?" I said I needed it two weeks ago, and he said, "But when do you absolutely, really have to have it?" I told him "Friday" and he promised me he would have the paint selected by Friday.

Well, Friday came and went with no paint selection. I called Randy on Monday, and he told me he had an emergency, which prevented him from making his paint selection, but he would have it to me by Wednesday.

At about 4:00 p.m. on Wednesday, Randy showed up and began to put samples on the wall only to find out he needed more samples to compare to his original samples. The next day more paint samples went up. Another Friday passed and Randy said he was having a difficult time making a decision.

In the meantime, we had already completed the drywall and work on the home was at a standstill. The process had lost momentum. I was frustrated, Randy was frustrated, Randy's wife was frustrated, and the painter was frustrated. Even the cabinet man was frustrated because now his schedule was delayed.

Everyone was frustrated and all the work had stopped.

The painter wasn't sure he wanted to sign up for my next job, and my reputation as a builder started to get a little shaky.

If you've ever built a home, you know it can be very frustrating and time consuming without the help of an interior designer. You take your paint color chip along with your carpet sample and drive across town trying to match your tile with a designer deco piece for your shower. Then you take those samples to the granite supply yard, drive back across town to a cabinet supply house, and swing over to the lighting store. Along the way you're bombarded with a plethora of opinions from all of the people working at all of those stores. It's not only confusing—it's exhausting!

If your builder does not have an in-house design team to help you in your selection process, then at least retain a competent interior designer who complements your style and, as difficult as it may be to make your selections before you begin your home, do it—for your benefit, your spouse's benefit, your family's benefit, and for the benefit of the builder's and your relationship.

If you do this before the construction begins, the only thing you'll need to select after that is your toothbrush. You'll be able to enjoy the building process, and your builder can build your new home more effectively.

BOTTOM LINE

For a more enjoyable (not to mention saner) building experience, make <u>all</u> your selections before construction begins.

The Startling Step Most New Homeowners Fail to Take

Obtaining feedback from previous homeowners is critical to selecting the right builder for your new custom home. It's a good idea for you to call a builder's previous homeowners to ask how he performed with their project. It's important to ask what the builder did very well and what some of his weaknesses were.

Of course, it's important to realize that one builder can't be all things to all people. Each builder will have some strong points, but they will also have some limitations as well. If you are looking for the "perfect" builder, I've got some bad news for you. One doesn't exist. However, if you're looking for a builder who's committed to excellence and integrity, and builds quality, custom homes, then such builders do exist.

Every builder has a unique background and unique strengths and limitations. Look for the things that matter: experience, excellence, integrity. Quality custom home builders know their own strengths and limitations. They don't shy away from them, but they work through them and provide excellent service and an excellent home—though not a "perfect" one.

Here are a few questions to ask a builder's previous homeowners:

❧ Did your builder finish your home on time? If not, why not?

❧ Did your home come in on budget?

❧ Was there ever a time you felt your builder was being untruthful?

❧ Did your builder communicate to you clearly if there were any additional charges that you would incur?

❧ What are your builder's best qualities?

❧ What are some of your builder's weaknesses and limitations?

❧ And the most important question: Would you have your builder build for you again the next time?

❧ BOTTOM LINE ❧

Talk to the builder's previous homeowners to understand his strengths and limitations. Also remember that no builder is perfect.

Will I Go over Budget?

If you're like most people, yes, you will probably go over your budget.

On the way home from work, I occasionally stop at the grocery store just to pick up a couple of quick items. As I get out of the car, I'm thinking I'll be in and out in five minutes.

Twenty minutes later, I'm standing in the checkout line, my arms filled with items I never intended to buy. The watermelon was on sale, the blueberries were a two-for-one special, there's a new brand of chips that looks delicious, and on it goes.

Now I'm standing in line with my arms and fingers filled with items wondering what I came here for in the first place. Oh yes, a gallon of milk and bananas! I have to set the items down and run back to the dairy department because I forgot the milk! Does any of this sound familiar? Most likely you've been there before. The same thing can happen with the new homebuilding process if you're not careful.

As you shop for the latest and greatest appliances, you may find it enticing to upgrade. After all, it's only another $840. And the carpet is only $2.00 more per square yard than your budget planned. Then you decide that you really need nicer plumbing fixtures, upgraded light fixtures, and so on. I've found that it doesn't matter how high the budget is we help establish for our homeowners. If you're not careful, you will quickly exceed your budget. If you have an appropriate electrical fixture allowance of $20,000, for example, and I increase it to $30,000, it's still easy to overspend.

Here's what I know: Even if we bumped up every budget by 30 percent, most people would spend more than their budget allowed.

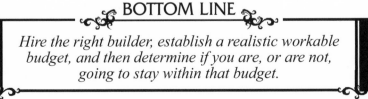

BOTTOM LINE

Hire the right builder, establish a realistic workable budget, and then determine if you are, or are not, going to stay within that budget.

How Many Bids Should I Get for My New Home?

Recently I met with Ross at a lot where he was considering building a new home. About 25 minutes into the meeting, I noticed he was distracted by a car that had pulled up to the property.

I asked Ross, "Are you expecting someone?" He told me he was meeting with *six* builders that day and requesting bids from all of them. As I wrapped up the final few minutes of our meeting, Ross asked if I could give him a bid on his new home. The plans weren't complete; there were a lot of items that needed to be corrected (the specifications, including the finishes, tile, cabinetry, countertops, etc., weren't even defined), but he still wanted a bid from me.

I followed up with a letter to Ross affirming that I thought it was a good idea for him to *interview* six builders, but from my experience getting six *bids* was counterproductive. When all the bids came back, there would be no common basis for him to compare what was or was not included in the bids. In other words, he would be comparing apples to oranges to potatoes to carrots to tomatoes, and this would only add to the confusion of an already involved process. I suggested that Ross narrow his scope down to one or two builders that he connected with and felt he could trust, like, and respect, and put focused energy in working through the details of his new home.

A few days later at a local builders' meeting, I ran into Steve, the builder who had arrived after me at Ross's lot that day. I asked Steve about his meeting with Ross, and he said the project was too crowded for him. Ross had also asked Steve for a bid, and Steve was going to pass.

I'm not advocating you only interview one or two builders, but I am suggesting you narrow your search down to one or two builders. When I know there are many builders competing for the same job (especially if the job doesn't have a clear, defined focus), I decide to put my limited time and energy where I can be most effective. That's with people who have narrowed their scope, have a reasonably good idea of what they want, and who value what I value. Then we can put more concentrated effort in to addressing their needs and concerns.

Quality, custom-home builders often don't have to bid their jobs against other builders because from the onset they have made a connection with the homeowner, discussed their fee structure, and demonstrated their competency. As a result, they can give their homeowners focused service. This is important because it takes a tremendous amount of time, energy, and focus to execute the process of homebuilding with excellence.

BOTTOM LINE

Interview builders first and select your builder based on trust and respect, not necessarily on the lowest bid.

Excellence or Perfection?

A prospective homeowner once asked me, "Will my new home be perfect?" I told him there are two kinds of perfectionists: one who asks for perfection but realizes life is not perfect and is very pleased with 95 to 98 percent. The other type expects perfection and is *never* happy, no matter how well a job is done.

If you are the latter, *please don't build a custom home.* Life is too short and too wonderful to take two years—or more—out of your life only to be disappointed in people and processes that are not perfect.

People build custom homes. *People* are not perfect.

It doesn't mean you can't or shouldn't expect *excellence*. Here are a few ways that excellence differs from perfection:

> Excellence is taking people and materials that are imperfect and executing a process to its very highest level.

> Excellence is a home that's done on time.

> Excellence is what happens when something goes wrong and it's quickly recognized and corrected. (Trust me, when you build a custom home, things will go wrong.)

> Excellence is when your builder acknowledges his mistake and promptly corrects it without pointing fingers.

> Excellence is clear communication.

> Excellence is a quality home built with straight walls, functioning doors, and overall good quality.

> Excellence is moving into your home and having your dishwasher, garbage disposal, and gas grill all operational on move-in day.

🔖 Excellence is a phone call from your builder if something unexpected comes up and the schedule needs to be modified.

🔖 Excellence is having a homeowner so pleased that when the topic of homebuilding comes up he says, "Let me tell you about my builder."

Planning, designing, and building a new custom home for you and your family can be an exciting, rewarding experience if you select a competent builder who is committed to *excellence* and you have a clear understanding of each other's expectations. Homebuilding can be a miserable experience if you are a perfectionist who is unhappy even if your builder builds to excellent standards.

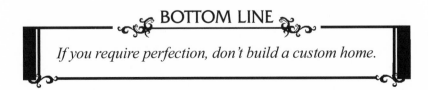

ᗒᔉ BOTTOM LINE ᔉᗕ

If you require perfection, don't build a custom home.

Why Picking the Right Builder
Is Half the Battle

How important is it to choose a good builder? It's #1 on the list!

You will have a lot of decisions to make as you build your custom home—selecting colors and finishes, determining size and layout, and more. But no decision will impact your homebuilding experience more than the all-important decision you'll make right at the start. You need to choose a great builder!

The fact is you can't do a good deal with a bad person. No matter how hard you work, you can't make a silk purse out of a sow's ear. The same is true with your builder. Here are the three most important qualities to look for in a builder for your custom home:

1. **TRUST:** Building a new home is probably one of the largest investments a person will ever make. If you don't believe your builder has your best interests in mind, you're talking to the wrong builder. You want a builder who works on your behalf, not someone who is only looking out for his own interests. When you call your builder, will you get a straight answer? If something goes wrong on your job, do you trust your builder to make it right? Believe me, when you build a custom home, there will always be bumps in the road no matter which builder you select. There isn't a contract written yet that will cover every possible condition that you may encounter while building your new custom home. Ask yourself: *What is your builder's intent?* If his internal compass is pointing north (with intentions to do the right thing, even when it's difficult), you're halfway there.

2. **COMPETENCE:** Does your builder have the ability to see and execute your home from start to finish? Is he able to walk you through the concept and design stage to produce a home that will reflect your needs, wants, and lifestyle? Does he have the right interior design team to complement your taste and preference? Does he have the right office staff that will politely and professionally respond to your needs and questions? Does he have an on-time, competent construction team to oversee the building of your new custom home? Does your builder

have systems and procedures in place that will allow him to execute the building of your home in an excellent way? Does your builder have a reputation and history in the community that speaks well of his business?

3. FAIR PRICE: Does your builder charge a fair price? Most people start by looking at cost first. While price is certainly important, it's not nearly as critical as trust and competence. That's why I put this quality last.

If you know your builder is charging you a fair price for his services, and if you know he is trustworthy and competent, *look no further*. You have found your builder. Hire him and begin to focus on how to make your dream home a reality.

BOTTOM LINE

Look for trust, competence, and fair pricing in selecting a builder to build your custom home.

What About Storage?

If you are like most Americans, you accumulate stuff. Stuff takes up space, sometimes a lot of space. Over the years, you may have accumulated things with sentimental value, seasonal items (decorations you use once a year), or extra playthings for those wonderful visits from the grandchildren.

In the homebuilding process, many people fail to take into account their need for storage, and if they do, they generally underestimate the amount of storage space they will need. In a new home design, people are generally willing to pay more for a home with adequate storage than a home with more finished space that's seldom used (e.g., extra bedrooms). Adding storage space can be accomplished in the early design stages if your builder knows this is a priority for you. The additional cost is minimal as long as your builder knows well ahead of time so he can direct the designer accordingly.

If you live in the north, you know that most homes are built with basements, which are an excellent place for storage. However, for homes along the coast, basements are rare; instead, attic spaces are often used. Some people want a separate structure, and storage sheds can be planned if requested. Another common storage solution is to create spacious walk-in storage closets within the home itself.

It's easy to create storage space in a walk-in, easily accessible, partially finished attic. Access is often located on the second story with entry from a common area such as a game room or shared space.

If you're building a one-story home, a common place for storage is the attic space above the garage. Your builder can make changes to roof framing to allow for light storage and easy access above the garage.

You should consider our country's demographics of an aging population, and be sensitive to the safety of using a pull-down ladder to access attic space. Upgrading these access ladders to light commercial aluminum ladders is money well spent for the safety and ease of access for you and for any future homeowners.

You can also design attic spaces above garages that have their own separate set of stairs. The stairs are much safer than pull-down ladders; they are often not carpeted and have a very simple handrail for safety. This is an additional, value-added benefit not only for the homeowners' safety but also for resale value.

It's important to think through your storage needs as you begin to design your new custom home.

✒ BOTTOM LINE ✒

Don't forget about storage. Tell your builder how much of a priority storage is to you and look for opportunities to create inexpensive storage space.

How Do You Avoid a Builder Scam?

W e hear of new scams all the time. You can hardly pick up a newspaper these days without reading about some unscrupulous people devising a new scam to take advantage of unsuspecting people. While this may be true, it doesn't mean *you* have to become a victim. Knowing what signs to watch for can help keep you out of trouble. Pay attention to these warning signs:

☛ TOO GOOD TO BE TRUE: When a builder gives you a price that sounds too good to be true, be wary. If a builder says yes to all of your questions, walk away. If you ask him if something is included in his price, and he ALWAYS answers yes, be cautious. It can't ALL be included! If it sounds too good to be true, it probably is.

☛ TOO FEW REFERENCES: If a builder is only willing to give you two or three references, you should wonder why. Any builder can give you a few references, although it may be his brother, cousin, and very best friend. Make sure the references you get are recent and credible.

☛ RUSH TO CONTRACT: If a builder is trying to get you to rush to sign a contract with him, you should see red flags waving and a caution light going off. Building a custom home is a big decision, and if you're rushed into signing something, you could be in for some big surprises later.

☛ CHECK ONLINE RESOURCES: There are online resources available where you can verify some important information on the builder. In some states, you can do online verification of a builder's credentials and license, verify how long he has been in business, the tax ID number, search for liens, find out if their workers compensation insurance is current or has ever been cancelled. Another good resource is your local Better Business Bureau.

VAGUE SPECIFICATIONS: If the specifications are vague (type of material, quality, and finishes for your home), and/or incomplete, ask that they be made specific. Vague specifications leave a lot of room for interpretation and are one way a scammer can argue later. If you sense your builder is being vague or giving you specifications that are incomplete, consider getting a bid from another reputable builder to compare the specifications from each builder. This will help you raise your level of confidence in the builder you choose that he is being honest and forthright about what he is and what he isn't providing in his proposal for your new home.

INSUFFICIENT ALLOWANCES: One of the most common ways that a builder could present a price that is too good to be true is to knowingly or unknowingly include allowances that are insufficient to complete your home as you expect it. The allowances provided should mean something to you. You should have a good sense as to what your allowances will buy. In researching your allowances, if you find that the level of quality that the allowances provide are consistently less than what you and your builder discussed, be wary.

A little healthy skepticism is a good thing. Respect and trust are earned and you want your builder to earn your respect. If you have any suspicions at all that a builder is trying to scam you, do not sign a contract with him, even if it means you have to start all over again with another builder. When it comes to building your new home, trust is everything.

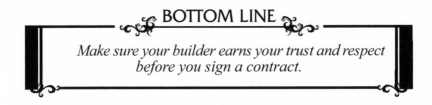

BOTTOM LINE

Make sure your builder earns your trust and respect before you sign a contract.

Financial Smarts
Where Do I Start?

W hen it comes to paying for your custom built home, do you know where to find your financing? Many don't. Should you peruse the Sunday papers looking for the best deal or stop by your neighborhood bank to see their rates? Do you need a mortgage lender or a mortgage broker? When it comes to finding the right home financing plan, it's really all about dollars and sense.

First, let's define the difference between a mortgage lender and a mortgage broker. Most mortgage lenders can be found at a banking institution. Their services are provided as a bank service. A mortgage broker, on the other hand, charges fees to go out and find a lender for you based on your specific financial qualifications. As a custom homebuyer, you should look for a loan officer who has experience in construction financing with the education and experience to match the banking institution. The best and most reputable lenders won't be found by scouring the Sunday papers to find the lowest rate. If you're seeking competitive rates among several lenders, don't just focus on the price. While one lender may offer a terrific rate, you may be sacrificing speed, service, or their ability to actually help you acquire a loan.

The best place to start is to ask your builder who he uses. Like his vendors and subcontractors, he should be working with a reputable competent loan officer. You may want to ask your friends for referrals as well. In these volatile market conditions, it's wise to have a trustworthy loan officer with sufficient experience to guide you down the path of one of the biggest financial decisions of your life. A good question to ask up front is whether the loan officer will be working with you during the entire process or will you get passed off to another person in another department.

Once you've narrowed your choice, you'll want to meet with your loan officer to determine what size loan you qualify for to build your custom home. You'll need to fill out a loan application that will focus on three key areas: your credit, your debt-to-income ratio, and your liquidity (assets and retirement reserves). While the application can be filled out and sent back by email or fax, it's probably better to take the time and fill out the forms in person. Block off at least an hour to do this and answer any relevant questions your loan officer may have. This is where all of your time spent organizing and filing will pay off. You'll need to bring the most recent copies of pay stubs, your W2 forms, and two previous years' tax returns.

Also bring your most recent statements of checking and savings accounts, retirement funds, IRA account information, and other assets that show your financial strength. Loan officers advise clients to disclose all of their assets on the application form to give the most flexibility in arranging loan approval.

One of the items that will determine your ability to obtain a loan is your credit score. A credit score is a number that is determined by the three major credit-reporting agencies (Experian, Equifax and TransUnion) and is based on historic and current data that determines your credit risk. These numbers are not set by the mortgage lenders or by the banks. Your credit report is your financial thumbprint: every purchase you've made, every bill you've paid (or didn't pay), and every loan you've applied for (car, mortgage, etc.) is logged on your credit report. A credit report is used to determine an individual's credit worthiness. Credit scores range from 300 to 850, and the higher your credit score, the more desirable you look to a financial institution for a loan. Keep in mind, the higher your credit score, the lower the interest rate you can probably get.

It is a good idea to check your credit report before applying for a loan to check for any inaccuracies, especially if you have a common name. Before applying, you may also want to pay down as many debts as possible to help improve your income ratios. Also, the major credit bureaus offer services that will educate you on how to increase your credit scores. They are the experts. Remember, your debt-to-income ratio and credit score are important factors when qualifying for a mortgage loan.

When you are ready to submit the completed application and supporting financial documents, **you may be required** to pay $300-$500 to process your application with the lender. Once all of your financial documentation is turned in and reviewed, the loan officer will submit the application to the underwriter for approval. It usually takes 3-5 days to hear whether you've been approved or denied for the loan. An approved loan will usually come back with a capped interest rate for a specific period of time (30, 60, or 90 days). Once you receive the call from your mortgage loan officer with the good news, you're on your way to the next step of the financial process.

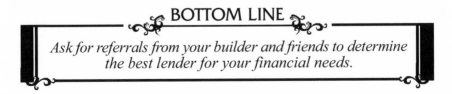

BOTTOM LINE

Ask for referrals from your builder and friends to determine the best lender for your financial needs.

What Kind of Warranty Can I Expect?

An important question to ask your builder within the first few meetings is, "What kind of warranty can I expect?" You'll want to know if he provides the minimum warranty allowed by law or if his reputation and written warranty exceed your expectations.

Most builders provide a one-year warranty on every home. But what's most important is what previous homeowners say about the warranty. The warranty can be an extension of marketing. It's a good idea to call the builder's previous homeowners and ask how your builder did with the warranty and if there was anything he refused to do for them. Did he exceed expectations not only during the warranty period, but did he also show a willingness to correct things beyond the warranty period?

We can make choices to handle things that are not required, and for this reason we continue to get referrals over and over again.

When someone buys a Lexus and something goes wrong with their car one day after the warranty expires, there's a good chance the dealership will do whatever is necessary to keep the customer happy. After all, people who buy a Lexus have different expectations than people who buy a Hyundai or a Chevy.

People spend their hard-earned money with us, and we work hard to exceed their expectations. Are we perfect? No. But I believe the sign of a great company is how you handle problems. We work very hard to exceed people's expectations.

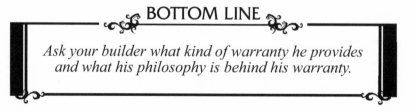

BOTTOM LINE

Ask your builder what kind of warranty he provides and what his philosophy is behind his warranty.

PART II

DURING
CONSTRUCTION

Don't Sweat the Small Stuff

A few years ago, Richard Carlson wrote *Don't Sweat the Small Stuff— and It's All Small Stuff.* In his now famous book, he said, "Often we allow ourselves to get all worked up about things that, upon closer examination, aren't really that big a deal..."

That's not only good advice for life, it's especially important during the homebuilding process. I can assure you, there's going to be a lot of small stuff during the building of your home.

Many people who frequently call their builder's office worrying about minor things make the building process much more difficult, both on the builder and on themselves. A homeowner who worries when a subcontractor is two hours late to the job, or needs to know why a two-by-four has a knot hole in it, or notices some sawdust in a corner of the living room can take the wind out of anyone's sail and cause delays.

Yes, it is important to let your builder know if there are things that truly concern you because your builder wants to provide a complete and pleasurable experience. However, people who view every little thing as a "big deal" and worry about it all (especially those who call their builder daily with their current worry list) are never going to be satisfied.

Jordan was someone who excelled in "sweating the small stuff" during the building of his new home. Throughout the design and contract stage of his new home, Jordan was a delight and seemed to be the perfect candidate for a successful project. The trouble started when his builder mentioned the surveyors were scheduled for Thursday. Even though the survey work didn't need to get done for at least two weeks, the builder wanted to schedule it early so it wouldn't be a critical component in the building schedule.

At 7:00 Thursday morning it was raining buckets and continued to rain all day. Early Friday morning, before the builder's offices opened, Jordan called because he was worried about the surveyor. The builder explained to him that because of the full day of rain the previous day, the surveyor was delayed by a day. Jordan was stressed. It was the first of many times throughout the process that Jordan was "sweating the small stuff."

A week later, when the material was dropped at his lot so construction could begin, the delivery truck got stuck due to all the recent rain. The builder's office got another call from Jordan wanting to know all the details about why there were tire ruts in his front yard.

The day the foundation man was scheduled he was delayed because of traffic. Another phone call from Jordan. Once the foundation work was prepared, Jordan called to find out what day the inspection would occur. Once inspection passed, Jordan wanted to know what the inspector said and why the inspection card in the permit box was signed off in black marker instead of blue ink.

After the foundation was installed, there was a bag and a half of mortar left over and two wheelbarrows of sand. Jordan called to ask what was going to be done with the leftover material.

It went on and on and on throughout the entire job! Jordan continued to "sweat the small stuff." No amount of meetings and explanations could convince Jordan to let the builder do what he had hired him to do. It was counterproductive to the relationship and impeded the builder's ability to execute the job with excellence. The builder spent more time answering Jordan's questions about the small stuff than he did looking for opportunities to build his home in the most efficient and effective way possible.

It's important to know that if you're going to sweat the small stuff (and remember, as Richard Carlson said—*it's all small stuff*), it usually will not help you get what you really want. At the end of the day, you and your builder both want the same thing: a quality, custom home completed on time and within budget. So relax and let your builder worry about the small stuff. In the end you'll be doing yourself a favor.

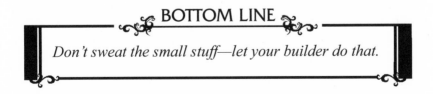

BOTTOM LINE

Don't sweat the small stuff—let your builder do that.

What Language Are You Speaking?

" I didn't buy this home at a scratch-and-dent sale. See that chip in my bathtub? I don't want it repaired. I want the entire tub torn out."

Rick clearly was not happy. He obviously had definite expectations and, in his opinion, they weren't being met.

It's imperative to have a clear understanding of your expectations if something is scratched or damaged during the construction process. There are over 100,000 components that go into a new, custom home, and in the process of installation, something may inadvertently get scratched or damaged. I recommend you agree in writing with the builder that if he can bring the damaged item to a new, quality standard, it will be mutually acceptable. If you took delivery on a new car and it had a minor scratch, you wouldn't expect the dealer to replace the entire door or the entire car. Agree on standards with your builder before you begin.

A builder friend of mine was once hired as a mediator to help resolve a conflict between a homeowner and a builder. Instead of going to a jury trial, the builder and homeowner had agreed to binding arbitration. The mediator's opinion would be binding.

When the mediator arrived at the house, he was introduced to Dr. Jones, the homeowner, who was already dressed for work in his medical scrubs. He was then introduced to Mr. Jenkins, the builder, who arrived dressed for work in his cowboy boots, blue jeans, and a Harley Davidson T-shirt. From the start, the mediator felt they were speaking different languages.

No wonder they had conflict! They came from two different worlds. The doctor was trained in exacting measures. He was trained to do things right the first time—every time. In his world, there were no second chances. A surgeon cannot tell a patient, "Oops, I forgot. I left a scalpel inside your stomach during the operation." But the builder in cowboy boots and blue jeans was thinking, *What's the big deal? The wall was put on the wrong side of the line. We can move it in ten minutes.*

Years later (and thousands of dollars in attorney fees later) there was the angry homeowner and the frustrated builder, each one looking for something the other could not provide. The surgeon was looking for a deal, and the builder was looking for the opportunity to say he built for a doctor.

In the end, the mediator provided his written binding judgment, but neither side ended up happy. The sad thing is all of this could have been avoided if they had understood what they didn't know about the other person's point of view.

I suggest you and your builder have your expectations defined and clearly written out before any construction begins. Building a new home involves so many components, and there will be things to deal with all along the way. Be clear how your builder will handle any issues.

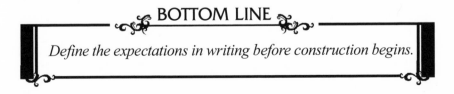

BOTTOM LINE

Define the expectations in writing before construction begins.

Eight Common Arguments Builders
Have with Homeowners
... and How to Avoid Them
—⟳🙟—

1. *Homeowner thinks: You never finished my punch-out, walk-through list.*

At closing, the builder and homeowner assemble a walk-through list. You walk through the entire house together to determine if there are any areas or items that still need attention. It's important to have this list in writing and signed by both the homeowner and the builder. If not, the list will never end. Your builder will become frustrated when items are continually added to the list; homeowners will be frustrated because they will feel as though the builder never completed the original list. Get the list in writing and agree that if any additional items arise beyond the initial walk-through, you will create a new, separate list.

2. Homeowner thinks: I didn't think adding two more windows to my new home would be an extra cost. After all, I'm paying a lot of money for this home.

Changes need to be clearly communicated *and* put in writing to protect both parties and the relationship.

3. Homeowner thinks: This is a shoddy builder. I never would've hired him if I had known this. Builder thinks: These homeowners have completely unrealistic expectations. I can never please them.

Before signing a contract, both the builder and homeowner need to clearly outline their expectations. While this may take a little more time, the effort is well worth it. Pen and paper up front can solve a whole host of misunderstandings and "he said/she said" situations down the line.

4. Builder thinks: The homeowner doesn't have sufficient funds to make changes. Homeowner thinks: The builder didn't communicate changes clearly and in a timely manner.

Agree in writing regarding any changes that occur after the contract is signed. I also recommend homeowners pay for changes they want at

Electrical Wholesale - Preferred Vendor - See Page 112

Johnson Brothers Planing Mill - Preferred Vendor - See Page 113

Architectural Elements and Design - *Preferred Vendor - See Page 110*

the time of the change, not at the end of a job. This will keep all parties on good terms with each other and the homeowner from having any big financial surprises at the end.

5. Homeowner thinks: My builder is not taking my concerns seriously; they are falling on deaf ears.

Have regularly scheduled meetings with your builder to update the schedule, changes, homeowner concerns, and items that the builder needs in order to complete the home. That way, you don't have to feel like you are nagging the builder and he doesn't have to feel like construction is being halted every time he turns around.

6. The homeowner says he spoke to the subcontractor, and the subcontractor said he could do something for the owner without the builder's knowledge.

All communication *must* be communicated through the builder or Construction Manager who is running the job. This will avoid "he said/she said" misunderstandings.

7. The homeowner is speaking to everyone but the builder on matters related to the home or its construction.

Open and honest communication with the builder or Construction Manager is vital, not just with anyone who will listen. Let the builder do what you hired him to do.

8. The homeowner is continually second-guessing the builder and the decisions he is making.

Take time at the start of the project to interview and gain a high level of trust with the builder and his abilities. Also, speak to previous homeowners about their homebuilding experience with this builder.

BOTTOM LINE

Save yourself headaches and heartaches by discussing all eight of these issues with your builder and resolve them in advance.

How Long Does It Take to Build a New Custom Home?

The amount of time it takes to build a new, custom home depends on the size, complexity, and geographic location (what part of the country you are building in).

The time it takes just to complete the architectural plans depends on how timely you make decisions and your availability to meet with your designer and builder for design meetings.

On average, developing a new set of plans that is ready for permitting can take between three and six months. Add one more month for permitting. For a home that's approximately 3,000 square feet, anticipate about an eight-to-ten month construction time, provided the market isn't overly busy and there is a timely response from vendors and subcontractors. If you're building a 6,000-square-foot home, anticipate a construction time of 12 to 13 months. For a 10,000-square-foot home, add two months to the design time and another six to eight months of construction time.

These estimates assume normal market conditions, which allow for a timely response from vendors and subcontractors.

It's important to understand the realistic timeline you get from your builder and the things that may delay a timely completion process. Help your builder keep the schedule by making your finish selections early. Beware of a builder who promises an overly idealistic timeline just to get the contract. In the end, you'll be stuck with the reality timeline.

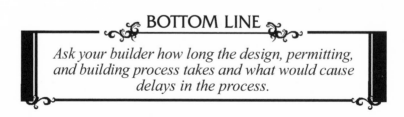

BOTTOM LINE

Ask your builder how long the design, permitting, and building process takes and what would cause delays in the process.

Understanding Two Worlds:
Yours and Your Builder's

I once talked to a builder friend who built a custom home for a world-class race car driver. The year my friend built the home, his client, Joe, was ranked number one in the world and won the driving circuit for that year.

Early on in the construction process, the builder couldn't understand why it was so unsettling to Joe if things didn't go quite as planned. If a subcontractor showed up a day late, even with a legitimate reason, Joe was upset. The builder began to feel somewhat disconnected with him.

Later that year, Joe gave the builder complimentary tickets to a big race. It was an exciting day with friends, watching the race from noon until 8:00 p.m., filled with the thrill of the race, the crowds, and the cars.

After heading home to bed, my friend woke up the next morning and turned the television on to see the latest report on this exciting 24-hour race. At that moment, the apparent disconnect suddenly made sense. After 21 grueling hours of racing, Joe was leading the race by a mere ten seconds!

It dawned on him at that moment—in Joe's world, ten seconds was everything. The precision required to be a world-class race car driver was very different than the precision required to build a home. To Joe, having a subcontractor show up a day late was incomprehensible. In this 24-hour race, Joe was part of a three-driver rotation. If, during the driver exchange, one driver bumps his knee on the door and loses four or five seconds in the transition, it can cost him the race.

The exacting standards of the construction industry were just *different* than the exacting standards of race car driving. Until that moment, the builder didn't understand Joe's world.

Before you enter into an agreement with your homebuilder, the two of you should seek to understand each other's worlds. If the builder had done this with Joe, it would have saved unnecessary turmoil in the building process.

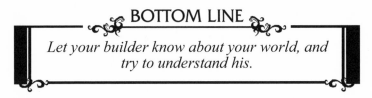

BOTTOM LINE

Let your builder know about your world, and try to understand his.

Should I Be Afraid of a Change Order?

No, you shouldn't be afraid of a Change Order—*if it's done right*.

What is a Change Order? Basically, it's a document that's used during the homebuilding process to let the builder know what you want to change from the original design specifications. For example, you may ask for a change because you want a different selection; you've changed your mind about countertops. Originally you wanted tile, but now you want granite. You can also use a Change Order to provide for a more functional use of space.

Your builder may also initiate a Change Order because material is no longer available, shipment delays have occurred, or a new and better product has become available.

The change listed on the Change Order must be described clearly with a fully researched price. Your signature will be required. A change may or may not affect the contract price of your home or the delivery date of the home. But, here's what really matters: You need to know! A Change Order does that.

So even if you initiate a Change Order for upgraded granite countertops and you agree to pay the extra cost, you still need to understand that shipping delays may bump the construction schedule back three weeks. Changes are possible, but they have consequences. The positive thing about a Change Order is everything is written down, you sign it, we sign it, and we're back in business. Nobody is going to hear "but I THOUGHT you said…" Changes are clear and documented.

Some homeowners may be afraid of a Change Order because most builders don't process them well. Can you imagine the chaos that would occur if we just proceeded with phoned-in instructions? You don't want to have a conversation with your builder where you both think, "but I'm *sure* he said…"

Whether the Change Order is a large or small item, it always creates a wrinkle in the construction process. Some section of work has to stop until we know if we need to change direction. We do research, make phone calls, and solicit new bids.

A Change Order may be due to a product being discontinued or there may be extensive delays in delivery of the original selection. Occasionally there are shortages of material and the builder may propose using another material in order to keep on schedule. This action would prompt a Change Order for you to review and sign. Remember, the Change Order protects you—it's YOUR home and you remain in the driver's seat.

BOTTOM LINE

Minimize the number of Change Orders by hiring a builder who communicates clearly upfront, before you start building. When a Change Order occurs, make certain a paper trail follows for your protection and the protection of your relationship.

Why Do I Have to Pay a Builder's Margin on a Change Order?

Homebuilders often hear, "Don't builders make enough profit so they can just include the changes as we go along? After all, we're building a custom home and we're entitled to make changes. Otherwise, we would've bought a home from a production builder."

While this seems like a valid point from a buyer's perspective, most people would be surprised to find out that builders don't make as much money as they think. We always encourage homeowners to work diligently on the front end (before construction begins) so they can keep Change Orders to a minimum. Changes can happen during the construction of a custom home, but you need to be aware of how the process works, the consequences of a change (additional time and cost), and understand the builder's margin.

Custom homes are built with as little as four changes and some with more than 200 changes. It's difficult to gauge how many changes a homeowner may make after signing the contract. Most people start out saying they love their plans and they love everything they've picked out. Yet once construction starts, we may receive nine phones calls requesting 20 changes during the first week alone!

Changes involve a lot of energy and a lot of the builder's team's time. In order to effectively process and execute changes to a custom home, a builder needs to be fairly compensated. The last thing that you want is to have your builder wincing when he looks at his mobile phone when you call. We're not saying that a builder should be able to take a trip to Hawaii because of a single Change Order fee he earns while building your home, but a fair and equitable fee that encourages your builder to work on your behalf for an excellent result is vital to the homebuilding process.

We don't encourage or discourage our homeowners to make changes. Being available to give professional counsel when questions about changes occur is our duty and responsibility. We're motivated to give our homeowners a great experience.

We once built a home for a corporate executive. John was a great client and a great guy. Our contract agreement outlined that he would provide his own refrigerator. Near the end of construction, John asked if he could use my supplier to purchase the refrigerator at my cost. Since we had a strong relationship and my focus was on serving, we allowed him to select the refrigerator. We had it delivered and only requested reimbursement of the cost of the appliance, without charging him a builder's margin.

In our original agreement, one of the items that this homeowner valued was an extended warranty, which we provided. Approximately fourteen months after John moved into his new home, the seal on the refrigerator failed and water leaked onto the hardwood floor, causing the floor to warp. When we contacted the appliance company, they indicated that the refrigerator was out of warranty and, since the home was still in warranty (because of the extended warranty period we had provided), we had an obvious problem. Not only did we have to pay to repair their refrigerator, but we also had to pay for repairing the kitchen floor and sanding and finishing the entire floor in his home because the new finish didn't match the original finish in the rest of the home.

We learned a valuable lesson from that experience. If changes occur that deviate from the original contract agreement, then a builder's margin must be charged to compensate fairly for the time, energy, and risk associated with items that may need to be addressed at a later date.

BOTTOM LINE

Agree in advance what the builder's margin will be on Change Orders. Decide what you want before construction begins, and if a change occurs, you'll have a mechanism that provides for a win/win situation.

How to Make Your Builder Love You
39

W e've built a lot of homes, and we've worked with some really great people and some very difficult people. Our most successful projects have been the result of developing strong relationships. Here are some tips on how to have a successful construction project and make your builder love you:

- ❧ TELL THE BUILDER WHAT HE'S DOING RIGHT. One particular homeowner found something good to say every time we spoke. Yes—*every time*. Nick didn't do this in a patronizing way; he gave me and my team genuine compliments. He looked for and commented on the positive aspects in our relationship and the services we were providing. Nick also shared his concerns with me. I would do anything for Nick and still would to this very day, more than five years after completing his home.

- ❧ CLEARLY COMMUNICATE PROBLEM AREAS. If something is bothering you about your new home construction process, clearly communicate what concerns you without anger or a condescending attitude. Give your builder an opportunity to make it right. A demonstration of a great builder is how well he handles problems.

- ❧ CLEARLY COMMUNICATE YOUR EXPECTATIONS. Be forthright and share with your builder what you really value and tell him what is important to you. If you're clear, you'll probably get what you want.

- ❧ LET YOUR BUILDER DO HIS JOB. We've been hired by homeowners in the past who seem to be agreeable, only to find out later they wanted to control the entire process and hover over us. Behavior like that makes our entire team reluctant to make a decision for them.

☞ THINK WIN/WIN. Builders are regular people just like your next door neighbors. They generally don't make as much money as people imagine, and most builders really want to do a good job. Work toward amicable solutions.

☞ REMEMBER TO SAY THANK YOU. Builders are people too, and everyone likes to hear a thank you for a job well done.

☞ PAYING ON TIME. Paying the contractor on time will allow subs and suppliers to be paid on time resulting in a smooth and more efficient project for you.

☞ KINDNESS. Sometime clients have provided donuts, snacks, or lunch on a Friday afternoon to subs and suppliers. This kind act can go a long way in keeping subs on the project and working harder to get the job done.

BOTTOM LINE

Follow these helpful hints and your builder will love you.

Why You Shouldn't Use Friends as Subcontractors

" I have a friend (or a brother-in-law) who is willing to do the tile work in my new home for a discounted rate. I'd like to use him and save some money."

Most quality custom home builders have learned the hard way that it's not a good idea to allow homeowners to use friends or relatives for subcontracting work on the house during construction. Frequently it turns out to be a disaster for both the builder and the homeowner. Here's one example of why:

Scott wanted to use his friend's custom cabinetry shop. Scott knew the friend well and had spoken to another friend who was pleased with the cabinetry from this particular company. The builder didn't want to allow it, but also didn't want to anger his client so he agreed to let Scott use his friend's cabinet company.

The builder was promised the cabinet work would be completed by a specified date, but the cabinets were not installed on time. In fact they were delayed several times and eventually caused a two-month delay in the construction schedule. In the end, Scott and his family moved in without any cabinet doors on the face of the cabinetry in their entire home and then waited an additional two months to have their job complete. That didn't even take into account the lost momentum or additional cost in interest carry, overhead, and other expenses as a result of the delay from the cabinet shop.

When you hire a builder, I strongly encourage you to allow your builder to do what he does best. When you visit a dentist, you expect him or her to be trained and equipped to do the job efficiently and effectively. You wouldn't think of bringing your own tools or materials, handing them to your dentist, and asking if you could save money on a filling because your neighbor or friend is in the dental supply business. You wouldn't take a steak to a restaurant and ask them to cook it for you so you could save a few dollars on the meal.

The principle is no different in homebuilding. If you use friends or your own business contacts, it will disrupt the smooth flow of work and communication of what an experienced builder does best. It could also produce conflict and put strain on your personal relationships. Trust your builder. He has vendors, subcontractors, and a labor force already in place that he works with on a regular basis.

⚜ BOTTOM LINE ⚜

Hire a competent builder to do the building; save your friends for the housewarming party.

The Top Eleven Mistakes Made by Homeowners

1. *Purchasing a lot that is "affordable."*

Solution: Remember: location, location, location. Purchase the most expensive, valuable lot you can manage, even if it means waiting on some finishes or amenities in your home. (See chapter 6 for more on this topic.)

2. *Trying to build a custom home without a professional builder.* Building a custom home is more complex than most people realize. It takes skilled professionals years to learn the business and even then changes in the industry, materials, and codes make it difficult to keep up.

Solution: Find a competent builder you can trust. Negotiate a reasonable fee for his services and hire him (see chapter 3).

3. *Purchasing a ready-made plan thinking it will save you money.* Building someone else's design or dream (especially one that was designed for someone in another city and state) may not be the wisest choice.

Solution: Purchase a ready-made plan only if your lot is standard and you don't need to modify the plan (see chapter 12).

4. *Choosing a builder primarily because of price.* The expression "you get what you pay for" applies to the homebuilding process. If you've heard horror stories about people's experience with their builder, it usually can be attributed to someone trying to get a deal.

Solution: Your home is a major investment. Make an informed, purposeful, thoughtful decision and don't be lured by the lowest bid (see chapter 17).

5. *Biting off more than you can chew.* In an appreciating market, the rise in value can cover this mistake, but in a flat or declining market, it can be disastrous.

Solution: Know what you can afford and stick to your budget (see chapter 23).

6. *Hiring a builder when your gut instinct tells you not to.*

Solution: After careful research and comparing builders, go with your instinct, not the discounted price (see chapters 4 and 28).

7. *Making choices for your home that only you love but everyone else hates.*

Solution: Get good counsel from your builder, designer, interior designer, and real estate professional before you make your decisions (see chapter 14).

8. *Expecting workers to be on your job every day from 7:00 a.m. until 4:00 p.m.*

Solution: Recognize that some days no work is scheduled at all because inspections may be taking place or rain has caused a change in the schedule (see chapter 31).

9. *Underestimating the importance of making all selections before construction.*

Solution: Make all selections prior to construction and enjoy the building process (see chapter 22).

10. *Homeowners giving direction to subcontractors on the job.*

Solution: Communicate only with the Construction Manager or builder. The Construction Manager is the only person on the job who has *all* the information related to your project. Subcontractors have only one piece of the puzzle. You can visit the job site during scheduled appointments with the Construction Manager who can answer your questions and explain what you will be seeing.

11. *Not understanding the "Change Order" process.*

Solution: Discuss the builder's Change Order process with him and be sure you are clear with how it works. Cooperating fully with this process will go a long way toward your enjoyment of the whole project (see chapter 36).

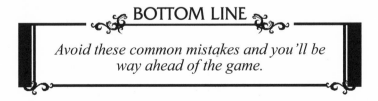

✎ BOTTOM LINE ✎

Avoid these common mistakes and you'll be way ahead of the game.

Should I Hire an Independent Building Inspector?

Sometimes homeowners choose to hire an independent building inspector during the building process of their new home, but that decision can be a double-edged sword.

On one hand, if the building inspector's intent is to genuinely help the process by effectively communicating what he observes, it can really aid in the process of completing a new home. On the other hand, a building inspector who tries to justify his fee by searching for insignificant things can add confusion and even create an adversarial relationship between the builder and the homeowner. When this happens, nobody wins.

We don't discourage our homeowners from hiring an independent building inspector. We think it's important for them to be fully comfortable with the building process. After all, they are investing a lot of money in their new home. If the homeowners can clearly define in positive terms what they want the inspector to do, the inspector will know we're not in an adversarial position. We will all be on the same page, working together to create a beautiful home.

Much of what is noted by a private building inspector is already being handled by the builder or the required local, county, and municipal building inspectors at code inspections. Hiring the private building inspector may be additional cost without any real value added to the homeowner.

Homeowners who live out of town, out of state, or even out of country from their homebuilding site may want to hire an inspector to watch over the construction process. This is a different assignment. To achieve the desired results, it will be important to choose a building inspector who understands the difference and does not try to create an adversarial situation. A good choice here can make or break a situation. We look for people who understand the "we're-all-on-the-same-team" mentality (and a lot of people don't). We're all on the same side; we all want the same thing. We all want a beautiful home, built to the highest standards. Our goals are not opposite yours or the inspector's. Understanding this is crucial. Be sure you are not hiring someone who feels the need to justify his fee.

For any homeowner, if you are feeling uneasy about your builder, then you should question why you are hiring that builder in the first place.

BOTTOM LINE

If you hire an independent inspector, make certain he is helping, not hindering, the building process.

How To Maximize Your
Valuable Investment
—❧—

You know how you feel when you drive a new car out of the showroom? You don't want any dust, dirt, or stains to ruin the beautiful seats on the inside or paint on the outside. You keep the interior clean and regularly wash and wax the exterior to keep it spotless. A little preventative care can go a long way in preserving the life of your new car. The car manual provides a maintenance plan that highlights key times to perform routine care to keep the engine running smoothly and the rest of the car performing at its peak.

Do homebuilders provide a similar maintenance plan to new homeowners letting them know what regular care should be given to their new home? Not usually. But they probably should. After all, a new home is one of the biggest investments most people make during their lifetime. So it's wise to take care of it from the start. A little planning and elbow grease will go a long way toward keeping your home clean, maintaining its value, and avoiding costly repairs later on. If you're not that handy around the house, you might want to consider hiring a professional to tend to things that need cleaning and maintaining. This will be money well spent.

Here is a home maintenance plan with some suggestions for maximizing enjoyment of your new home and maintaining its value.

- ❧ CLEAN THE GUTTERS AND THE FILTERS: Have your home's gutters cleaned at least twice a year to avoid leaf buildup. Also be sure to change (or clean if they are reusable) your air conditioner's filter every three months. A clean filter helps your unit run more smoothly and saves you money on your electric bill. A clean filter also increases the life of your air conditioning unit. Nothing is more frustrating (not to mention costly) than having to install a new air conditioning unit in the middle of the summer.

- ❧ REPLACE WITH FRESH BATTERIES: Daylight-savings time is a great reminder for this step. In the fall and spring, when you adjust your clocks, replace the batteries in your smoke alarm. As an extra note, be sure to check your irrigation clock every few months to ensure proper operation.

AVOID ABRASIVE CLEANERS ON HARDWOOD: If you have hardwood floors, it's important to keep them clean in order to extend their beauty and life. However, be careful to never use wax or harsh cleaners on your hardwood floors. The chemicals could permanently damage the flooring and result in a costly fix.

GARAGE DOOR SAFETY REMINDERS: Two important things to keep in mind if you have a garage door opener. First, never remove the garage door obstruction sensor. This safety feature is designed to prevent the overhead door from coming down on a child or animal and injuring or killing them. Check the sensor every few months to make sure it is working properly. Second, it's important to never try any type of garage door spring maintenance or adjustments by yourself. If the tightly coiled spring somehow comes off, it can cause serious injury. Always hire a trained installer or maintenance professional to assist you.

CHECK AND RESEAL: Check the exterior of your home twice a year for any signs of expansion or contraction. Cracks may allow water to seep in causing extensive damage to the interior walls. Caulk cracks and seal wood to prevent future problems.

While this maintenance plan is not comprehensive, it does include some of the most important items every homeowner should do to protect their investment. Your home may have some additional needs to consider.

Why not take this maintenance plan and find a creative way to remind yourself to do these activities. Perhaps you could write reminders on your wall calendar, schedule them into your Day-Timer, or set up reminders that will pop up on your computer. However you decide to do it, these regular maintenance items will maximize your home's value and maintain its beauty for years to come.

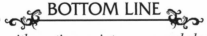

BOTTOM LINE

Keep up with routine maintenance and cleaning around your house or consider hiring professionals to protect your new home investment.

What Can I Expect After I Move In?

—⊷⊱⊷—

Imagine it's been a few months since your custom-built home was completed. You've moved the furniture in, decorated your favorite spots with mementos and other personal belongings, and even hosted a few housewarming and dinner parties. Your home is the envy of the neighborhood and your friends marvel at the attention to detail and excellent craftsmanship. But there are no perfect homes, and a fact of new home construction involves the foundation settling and minor cracks appearing. Many of the cracks appear because your home is adjusting to temperature and humidity changes—builders can't build your home under factory-controlled conditions. So don't panic when minor cracks appear. This is completely normal!

To help ease your fears, here's a list of common situations that occur in new homes. Builders are often asked these questions (and plenty more) from panic-stricken homeowners who fear their perfect home is now laden with problems. Remember, thousands of components were used to put together your home over an extended period of time, so settling and minor adjustments should be expected. A good builder will address your concerns promptly and work with you.

So what can you expect?

⊷ **CROWN MOLDING CRACKING:** This is very common and there's no way around it. Expect to find minor cracking and separation in your crown molding, especially in two-story homes. Settling, heat expansion, and contraction will occur as your home acclimates to the new temperature conditions inside from running your air conditioner and heating systems. This *does not* mean there is anything structurally wrong with your home. Cracks in your crown molding actually look worse than they really are. A qualified handyman can caulk these minor cracks within minutes, and after the repair you shouldn't be able to tell there was ever a crack at all.

⊷ GROUT CRACKING: Another common spot to find minor cracking is in the tub and shower area. You may notice cracks appearing along the grout lines between tiles or in the corners of the tub or shower. Again, a handyman with the appropriate sealant can take care of this. It's a good idea, however, to add the sealant quickly to prevent moisture from seeping behind the tile and causing further damage.

HARDWOOD EXPANSION AND CONTRACTION: If you have hardwood floors professionally installed in your home (not constructed from a pre-fabricated kit), you can expect to find some minor cracks appearing over time. The hardwood acclimates to the temperature of your home (again due to cool air and heat) after installation and the wood planks will expand and contract. This is normal! It's best to allow the wood to expand and contract for at least six months so it completely settles before making any repairs. A professional installer or handyman can putty in the minor cracks.

DOOR ADJUSTMENTS: Even doors and door frames will need time to adjust to the temperature after a new home is finished. The doors, locks, door handles, and deadbolts may need some minor adjustment. This is completely normal.

CRACKS IN THE SIDEWALK, DRIVEWAY, AND GARAGE: It is not uncommon for minor cracking to occur along concrete sidewalks, driveways, and even inside the garage. Expansion and contraction also happens here because of the varying temperature conditions that the concrete is exposed to. As long as you don't notice a difference in the height of the concrete on either side of the crack, don't worry. These cracks are normal. It does not mean that there is anything wrong with the concrete foundation. Typically cracks in concrete are not mended unless there is a height difference between the concrete on either side (see builders warranty for specifics).

RECEPTACLE NOT WORKING: If a receptacle (wall plug) in the bathroom, kitchen, garage, or in the home's exterior mysteriously stops working, don't be alarmed. It may just be a tripped circuit. The current electrical code requires builders to put in a receptacle called a GFI, or Ground Fault Interrupter. This measure is added for your safety to prevent accidental electrocution. These receptacles have an internal trip circuit built in that acts as a safety mechanism when there is water and electricity coming in contact. If there is an electrical surge, the receptacle will trip the GFI and automatically cuts off the electricity. Since four or five receptacles can be located on one circuit, it may be necessary to reset it. You'll need to look for a small button on the receptacle and push it. The button is usually located on the bottom or near the bottom of the receptacle site. If your receptacle continues to trip on a regular basis, call your builder or electrician to check out the problem.

This is by no means a complete list of situations that may occur after you move into your home. If you have a more specific question or situation, contact your builder to determine the best approach to fix the problem.

BOTTOM LINE

Some settling is likely to happen after you move in to your home, and some cracks may appear. Don't panic. The fix is usually easy, and it doesn't mean you have a defective house.

Is Going "Green" the Way to Go?

Today many builders and home buyers are concerned about preserving the environment. With increased attention on the condition of our planet, "green building" has become a sought after choice for homeowners.

But what does green building mean? In its simplest terms, green building is making your home more environmentally friendly. It means increasing your home's efficiency so it makes better use of things like water, energy, temperature control, and construction materials. It's about using resources effectively so you reduce the impact of your home on the environment.

While building an environmentally friendly home sounds good to most people, they usually want to know two things: what can I do and how much will it cost me? Let's address the last question first.

You may have heard that building green is more expensive. While that may be true in some instances, it doesn't have to be. In today's market some elements of green building can cost more initially, but many do not, and some even cost less. Factor in energy savings over time and the increased durability of many of the green building products, and any additional up-front cost becomes much easier to justify. Also, many mortgage companies now offer reduced mortgage rates to homes built green.

To answer the other question, let's take a look at a few things you can do to make your new home more environmentally friendly.

> ☙ HEATING AND COOLING EQUIPMENT: One of the most important things you can do to make your home more "green" is to carefully consider your choice of heating and cooling equipment. The heating / air conditioning system should be built and installed with the highest SEER (Seasonal Energy Efficiency Ratio) rating possible. The greater the SEER rating, the more energy efficient your unit will be.

The system should also be sized appropriately to effectively cool or heat your home without being oversized. In fact, it is often better to err on the side of being undersized by half a ton than oversized. (Note: A "ton" is a unit of energy used to measure output. Typically you need about one ton of output for every 400 square feet of your home.) Many builders don't recommend that you oversize the tonnage of your home's AC system. The most efficient homes often run on a system designed to be 10 percent smaller than typical installations. A good air system should also be installed with as few bends and connections in the duct work as possible to minimize the risk of gaps and voids.

❧ **INSULATION:** If it's within your budget, one great option is to have your home insulated with a foam product. When installed correctly, foam can be quite effective. On top of the good R-values (a term used to measure how well insulation resists the flow of heat or cold through it) foam can fill cracks and crevices in ways that traditional insulation can't. If a foam product can't be used, great care should be exercised to make sure the installation is done to eliminate as many gaps and penetrations as possible.

❧ **HOME ORIENTATION:** To reduce energy loads, it's important to design and position the house in such a way as to minimize exposure to the hot sun while taking advantage of cooling breezes. Whenever possible, the front door or the house's longest wall should be set to within 5 feet of true south. It may also be important to landscape in such a way to create wind breaks for the home or create shade to increase efficiency. Good window placement can increase natural light while reducing the need for electric lighting.

❧ **WINDOWS AND DOORS:** Windows help make a home beautiful, but they can also waste a lot of energy if they let in heat in the summer, cold in the winter, and drafts anytime. To get more energy-efficient, select windows with good insulation values. Some have special coatings that can help repel heat. Others are double-

or triple-paned which helps insulation. Some energy-efficient windows have non-toxic gas between the panes such as argon or krypton that provide better insulation than air. Even the window frames can affect how efficient they are. For example, aluminum frames typically provide the lowest insulation level. Wood, vinyl, and fiberglass are better. Warm-edge spacers are even better. Certain window coverings like reflective blinds and shades can also generate incredible savings on energy usage.

When it comes to doors, make sure they have a tight fit and use excellent weather stripping. Some new door frames include a magnetic strip that creates a tighter seal and reduces the amount of air that leaks out. Some of the best core materials for a door include fiberglass and foam. If a door has glass, it will be more energy efficient if double or triple-paned insulating glass is used.

ROOFING AND EXTERIOR PAINT: Consider using reflective roofing and lighter exterior paint colors. These two items offer a cooler home by reflecting the sun's rays rather than absorbing them. Roof choices (reflective) and lighter paint colors can create double digit drops in exterior surface temperatures which can result in greater energy savings.

BUILDING MATERIALS: Choose to use "earth-friendly" products and building materials whenever possible. Typically, these include:
– products made with recycled content
– products that conserve natural resources
– products that avoid toxic emissions
– products that are rapidly renewable such as bamboo, cork and
  straw.

WATER SYSTEMS: Consider installing tankless and "point-of-use" water heating systems. These systems do away with the traditional standing hot water tanks and more efficiently heat water for the home. They are also more cost effective.

➤ **APPLIANCES:** Consider installing "Energy Star" rated appliances. Energy Star is a program backed by the government that identifies products with high energy efficiency. These products often last longer and are more economical to operate than non-Energy Star rated appliances.

➢ BOTTOM LINE ➣

Building an environmentally friendly home can not only save you money over time, but also helps save the environment. But keep in mind, incorporating green features into you home early is critical to its success.

PART III

HELPFUL CHECKLISTS

This book would not be complete without a *"Helpful Checklists"* section. Each checklist is designed to make it easy for you to keep on track throughout the entire homebuilding process. You may want to review the lists and check off the items as you go through each phase. It can be helpful to take them with you to meetings with your builder or to the building site.

Your builder may have his own checklists for various stages of the design and build process. While they may differ in some details, they will most likely be quite similar.

These checklists have been helpful and valuable to our homeowners and to our company. They allow us to verify items that are significant in the design and construction process and make the process more efficient.

The following checklists are not exhaustive; they simply highlight some of the "must do's" while your new home is being built. We hope these tools will help you in your homebuilding experience.

CHECKLIST #1
Top Questions To Ask a Potential Builder

- [ ] 1. Why should I hire you?
- [ ] 2. What is your fee structure?
- [ ] 3. How do your fees compare to other builders?
- [ ] 4. What are your weaknesses?
- [ ] 5. What makes you different from other builders in this market?
- [ ] 6. What type of warranty do you provide, and what is your philosophy on warranty?
- [ ] 7. What was your worst building experience with a homeowner, and what did you learn from it?
- [ ] 8. How long have you been building?
- [ ] 9. What is your education?
- [ ] 10. How many custom homes have you built?
- [ ] 11. What is a custom home to you? When it comes to finishes can I select anything I want or will my selections be limited?
- [ ] 12. How many homes will you have under construction at the time my home will be built?
- [ ] 13. How many homes do you build per year?

☐ 14. How do you handle changes?

☐ 15. How many Change Orders would you consider average in building a home?

☐ 16. Do you supervise the building yourself, or do you have a site supervisor?

☐ 17. Can I meet the person who will be running my job?

☐ 18. How much time will you and/or your site supervisor spend exclusively on my job each week?

☐ 19. What work do you do with your own crews, and what work do you subcontract out?

☐ 20. Do you have contracts with your subcontractors? Can I see a sample?

☐ 21. Can you provide us with a bank reference?

☐ 22. Can you provide us with a copy of your insurance certificate?

CHECKLIST #2
What To Do Before You Hire a Builder

☐ 1. Look at some of the builder's homes currently under construction.

☐ 2. Look at some of the builder's completed homes.

☐ 3. Have the builder provide a list of previous homeowners.

☐ 4. Call two or three previous homeowners this builder has worked for and ask them key questions (see Checklist #3).

☐ 5. Become comfortable with the contract documents before signing.

☐ 6. Decide on your homebuilding budget.

☐ 7. Obtain a detailed budget or cost breakdown from each builder and compare to see that they are bidding the same items.

☐ 8. Ask for a list of several suppliers and subcontractors that the builder uses. Call at least three of them to see if the builder pays his bills on time.

☐ 9. Ask the builder how often he updates your budget to account for change orders and any cost overages.

CHECKLIST #3
Top Questions To Ask Your Builder's Previous Homeowners

—————

- ☐ 1. Why did you select this builder?
- ☐ 2. Did your builder demonstrate character and integrity during the time you knew him?
- ☐ 3. Did you feel your builder had your best interests in mind?
- ☐ 4. How well did your builder communicate Change Orders to you?
- ☐ 5. Did your builder treat you in a respectful, honorable way, and did he communicate clearly with you?
- ☐ 6. What was the worst thing that happened during your building process?
- ☐ 7. What would you do differently if you had to build your home all over again?
- ☐ 8. Was your home built on time?
- ☐ 9. Was your home completed on budget?
- ☐ 10. Was there ever a time you felt your builder was being untruthful?
- ☐ 11. Did your builder exceed your expectations?
- ☐ 12. What were your builder's best qualities?
- ☐ 13. What were some of your builder's limitations and weaknesses?
- ☐ 14. Would you use this builder again? (The most important question of all!)

CHECKLIST #4
Before You Begin Construction
—⁓⁓—

Review the following items with your builder at the job site before construction begins. This is not intended to be an exhaustive list; it includes the main things to check before you begin. Ask your builder to explain any items not clear to you.

☐   1.   Verify with your builder the height of the finished floor and all porches.

☐   2.   Verify with your builder the type of material used on all porches.

☐   3.   Verify with your builder all floor outlet locations.

☐   4.   Verify any recessed shower/tile locations.

     5.   Verify with your builder all hose bib locations.

☐

☐   6.   Verify with your builder electrical meter locations.

☐   7.   Verify with your builder layout and location of driveway and sidewalks.

     8.   Verify with your builder well and septic locations (if applicable).

☐

☐   9.   Verify with your builder pool equipment location (if applicable).

☐   10. Verify air conditioning locations. Is the unit too close to the master bedroom window?

     11. Verify that lot drainage conditions are correct.

☐

CHECKLIST #5
Before Your Builder Hangs Drywall
—ཀ༄—

Review the following conditions at the job site with your builder prior to hanging drywall:

———————————————————————ཀ༄—

☐ 1. Spot check room dimensions with your builder.

☐ 2. Verify with your builder that all closets are in place. These are easily overlooked by the framing contractor.

☐ 3. Review all door swings with your builder with electrical switch placement in mind.

☐ 4. Verify with your builder location and quantity of all electrical outlets, switches, cable TV, computer, etc.

☐ 5. Verify with your builder placement of breakfast nook ceiling fixture.

☐ 6. Verify any additional electrical outlet needs with your builder such as sockets, switch lights or holiday lights, receptacles, or convenient overnight mobile phone charging locations.

☐ 7. Review with your builder placement of master shower valves for easy reach to avoid scalding.

☐ 8. Verify cabinet layout and sink locations with your builder.

—ཀ༄———————————————————————

CHECKLIST #6
3 Weeks Prior to Closing

□   1.   Call your insurance agent to put homeowner's insurance in effect.

□   2.   Call your builder to verify the tentative walk-through date.

□   3.   Call electric company to schedule service in your name.

□   4.   Call telephone company to activate telephone service.

□   5.   Call cable company for TV hook-up.

□   6.   Call water municipality to schedule water in your name.

□   7.   Call gas company to schedule gas service in your name.

□   8.   Call lawn service company to put contract in place.

CHECKLIST #7
The No-Sweat List for Closing and Final Walk-Through
—◦୨ঙ৹—

This checklist will guide you through the process of what will happen on that long-awaited day—your closing day! After many months, it is finally time to hand you the keys. One of the important closing day events will be for your builder to walk through the entire home with you. This is an opportunity for the builder to instruct you about certain aspects of your new home and to point out locations with critical information.

A good builder will have his own checklist, but this list will let you know what to expect, and you can check off your own items as you walk through your beautiful, new, custom home together. It's also a great time to ask any questions.

- ☐ 1. Verify that keys work in every lock throughout the entire home.

- ☐ 2. Obtain garage door openers.

- ☐ 3. Obtain all extended warranties.

- ☐ 4. Obtain owner's manuals for all appliances.

- ☐ 5. Run the dishwasher through a cycle to be sure it works and there are no leaks or other problems.

- ☐ 6. Verify garbage disposal operation.

- ☐ 7. Verify gas hook-up to all appliances.

- ☐ 8. Verify hot water heater and recirculating pump operation.

- ☐ 9. Learn location of all air conditioning filters.

- ☐ 10. Locate emergency water shut-off valve.

- ☐ 11. Obtain subcontractor emergency phone numbers and information.

- ☐ 12. Obtain all final waiver of lien notices.

- ☐ 13. Obtain the Certificate of Occupancy.

☐   14. Obtain final Change Orders calculations.

☐   15. Obtain an updated list of all colors and finish selections.

☐   16. Verify pool is in working order (if applicable).

☐   17. Verify gas grill is working.

☐   18. Obtain home warranty.

☐   19. Schedule a 60 day walk-through follow-up date with your builder.

The Savvy Homeowner's Glossary
45 Indispensable Words Every Homeowner Should Know and Understand

—◦&◦—

1. **Adjustable Rate Mortgage (ARM):** A mortgage interest rate that changes based on an index over time.

2. **Agreement of Sale**: A sale contract.

3. **Amortization Schedule**: A schedule showing how the monthly mortgage payment is applied to the principal, interest, and the current mortgage balance.

4. **Appraisal**: An evaluation of homes within the surrounding area to determine the market value of the property.

5. **Appreciation**: An increase in the value of property.

6. **Borrower:** The person or persons responsible for the loan, also called the mortgagor.

7. **Cash Reserve**: The cash balance a borrower has left after closing, available for the first one or two mortgage payments.

8. **Certificate of Occupancy**: A certificate issued by a governing agency stating that the building has been approved for occupancy.

9. **Closing:** Finalizing the purchase and financing documents and the disbursement of funds to all parties.

10. **Closing Costs**: All the costs associated with the loan and the purchase, not including the actual cost of the property.

11. **Commitment Letter**: Formal notification from a lender stating the terms of the loan.

12. **Contingency**: A specific condition to an agreement or contract.

13. **Credit Report:** A report of credit history used to determine an individual's credit worthiness, usually provided by a credit bureau.

14. **Debt-to-Income Ratio**: The percentage of one's earnings used to qualify for a mortgage.

15. **Earnest Money**: A deposit given to a seller by a prospective buyer.

16. **Easement**: A right-of-way given to others to access over and across the property.

17. **Equity**: The difference between the market value and the outstanding mortgage balance.

18. **Fixed-Rate Mortgage**: A mortgage in which the rate of interest is fixed for the entire term of the loan.

19. **Flood Insurance**: Insurance for properties in designated flood areas by the government.

20. **Hazard Insurance**: Homeowner's insurance.

21. **Homeowner's Warranty**: Insurance that covers repairs for the home for a specified period of time.

22. **Lien:** A legal claim against a property that must be paid when the property is sold.

23. **Loan-to-Value Ratio (LTV):** The difference between the mortgage amount and the value of the property. Example: Home Value = $1,000,000; Mortgage amount = $900,000; LTV = 90%.

24. **Lock-in Rate:** A written guarantee by lender for a specific rate of interest.

25. **Mortgage Broker:** A company that matches borrowers with lenders for a fee.

26. **Mortgage Insurance**: Insurance that is provided by independent insurers that protects the lender in the event of a mortgage default.

27. **Mortgagee**: The lender.

28. **Mortgagor:** The borrower.

29. **Origination Fee:** The fee paid to a lender for processing a loan, also called points.

30. **Owner Financing**: When the seller of the property provides all or part of the financing.

31. **Plot Plan:** A map prepared by a licensed surveyor depicting the exact placement of a house on a lot.

32. **Points:** One-time charge by a lender. One point is one percent of the mortgage amount.

33. **Prepayment Penalty:** Fees charged to a borrower for paying off a loan prior to the maturity date.

34. **Pre-Qualification**: Pre-determining a buyer's financial borrowing power prior to a purchase. Pre-qualifying does not guarantee loan approval.

35. **Principal:** The total loan amount borrowed or the total unpaid balance of the loan.

36. **Radon:** A radioactive gas which, if found in sufficient levels, can cause health problems.

37. **Refinancing**: Paying off an existing loan with a new loan on the same property.

38. **Settlement Sheet**: The costs payable at closing to determine the seller's net proceeds from the sale and the buyer's required net payment.

39. **Survey**: A drawing showing the legal boundaries of the property.

40. **Title**: A legal document establishing the right of ownership.

41. **Title Company:** A company that specializes in insuring the title to the property.

42. **Title Insurance:** Insurance that protects the buyer and the lender against losses arising from disputes over ownership of the property.

43. **Title Search**: A search of legal records to ensure that the seller is the legal owner of the property and that any liens or claims against the property are identified.

44. **Transfer Tax:** State or local taxes due when title to property transfers from one owner to the other.

45. **Underwriting:** The process of evaluating a loan application to determine whether or not it's acceptable to the lender.

A FINAL THOUGHT

While building trends may come and go, one thing will always remain constant for us: personal relationships. The friendships and relationships we have formed in life are the one thing that sustains us–they truly speak to the heart and enrich our lives every day. The relationships that we formed early on still play a pivotal role in our work and personal life today.

We would not be where we are today without the faith, love and support of our family. Brent and I were lucky enough to have our father guide us and serve as a great role model and mentor. A father-son relationship is one of the most important relationships in a family and our bond was very strong. We've worked alongside Dad since we were young children. When there was a problem or question that came up during a project, Dad would ask us for our opinion on what should be done. Even at that early age, those moments had a profound impact on us and helped instill confidence in our abilities to succeed. Dad's faith in our work helped Brent and I grow into strong, independent men who wanted to bring those same values and principles of hard work and integrity into our own company. Even today, we often consult with Dad about our work because we still value his opinion and philosophy. Those life lessons that we learned are something we'll never forget and we hope to pass on those values to the next generation of Johnson builders.

B&B Builders doesn't just build homes for individuals. We build homes that become part of the community and part of a family's life story and history. Every home we build is one-of-kind and we are always happy for our customers and humbled by the experience every time we complete a home. Building a home is a stressful time for everyone–from the building crews to the homeowners–but we always remain friendly and eager to help our clients every step of the way. We want to assure them that by working together we can handle the challenges that are a part of building a custom home. For most people their home is the single biggest investment they will ever make. We want our homeowners to choose a builder that has their best interests as their goal. The ultimate compliment we can hear at the end of a successful project is a client to say, "Wow, this is better than I ever dreamed it would be."

Memories. That's what building a home is all about. Since 1993, B&B Builders has had the privilege of creating some of the most beautiful and distinctive homes for dozens of clients. Every day we meet people who are impressed with our detailed craftsmanship, impeccable architectural design, state-of-the-art techniques, and the ability to truly customize a home to their specifications. Our level of personal service, attention to detail, communication, high standards, and the ability to offer the highest possible quality at the lowest possible fair and honest price makes B&B Builders one of the top builders in the community.

Our hope is that after reading this book, you will move one step closer to custom designing your own dream home. A little pre-planning and really asking yourself if you have the time to devote to building a custom home can make the road to building your dream home run much smoother. Now that you know what's involved and you are armed with the knowledge to make better decisions, you can find a great builder to make your family's dreams come true. We would be honored to build those memories with you.

Ben and Brent Johnson

APPENDIX I
Pre-Construction Meeting
—❦—

As a contractor, we deal with many problems and concerns on each project. These problems and concerns are also unique to each project. What was important to our last client may not be important to you. Below are samplings of challenges and concerns that may impact your project. The purpose of reviewing these items is to clearly communicate expectations for your project before construction begins and to identify your concerns as well as what is important to you.

1. **Compaction** – Un-compacted fill around foundation walls, utility trenches or other filled areas will settle. Compaction isn't included in the contract except as required for structural footings unless specifically noted on the plans or in the contract documents.

2. **Positive Drainage** – It's the homeowner's responsibility to maintain proper positive drainage away from the house. Improper drainage can cause settling and lead to water leaking through the foundation. This settling can also lead to sidewalk and patio failure.

3. **Concrete** – Minor cracks in concrete are common and are not considered to be a defect. Concrete slabs will crack. Most concrete will crack. Concrete reinforcement, steel rebar, synthetic fiber, wire mesh and proper site preparation will help control the cracking.

4. **Designs** – There are literally thousands of ways to construct any given item in a home. At B&B we work very hard to ensure that the end product turns out as you envisioned it. Our understanding of what you want may not always be exactly the same as what you understood. If you have a specific idea of how you would like something done, please provide us with a photo and/or drawings and information to make sure we completely understand what you want. The more detail that you give us in a drawing, photo, material, dimensions and etc, the better chance we will have to do it right the first time. If something turns out different than what you wanted, we will redo the work at your request but reserve the right to charge for the additional work.

5. Special Order Materials – Note that many of the materials used in your home will be special order items. These items can have long lead times which can affect the completion date so make your finish selections early. Also understand that most special order items require a deposit at the time of order and in some cases can't be returned if you change your mind after they have been ordered.

6. Communication – Communication is key to any successful project. Regularly scheduled job walk throughs, email, cell phones and faxes will all play a part in communication for your project. In addition to these forms of communication, B&B has developed a web-based RFI system, which greatly enhances project communication when used properly.

7. RFI Log – To help verify that the hundreds of selections made during the construction process are made correctly, B&B has implemented a web-based RFI (Request For Information) log. In some cases, a RFI will be initiated if we have a question for you, such as, "Select Interior Door Style". In other cases, a RFI will be used to clarify and verify changes and/or verbal design selections you make. You will be given a log-in ID to review and answer RFI questions. Any selections or changes made by email, phone, or during a job walk through will be posted as a RFI on this web-based log. You will be notified by email about any new or updated RFI. We will do our best to accurately describe the design selection or change as we understood it. Please take the time to review each RFI and verify that our understanding is what you really want. Your prompt review, answer and approval of a RFI will help your project stay on schedule and ensure that the final product is what you wanted.

8. Owner Selection Form – As part of the design process, the RFI log helps to ensure that the many finishes selected during the project are correct. We will also provide you with an "Owner Selection Form" in phases so, final selections can be made as needed. Your prompt and accurate use of this form will facilitate keeping your project on schedule, within budget and can result in cost savings.

9. Natural Finishes – Many of the products we use in our homes have natural finishes. These natural finishes are unique, and in some cases, a living finish that will change over time. Samples are not always an exact duplicate of the actual finish you will obtain in your finished product.

Stone, Wood Siding, Roofing Materials, Concrete, Travertine or Slate Tile, Wood Doors & Trim, Cabinet Finishes and Bronze Hardware are all examples of natural finishes. If you have specific finish requirements in any area please let us know and we will make an extra effort to ensure that the correct finish is obtained. For example, stained alder has a tendency to be blotchy. We try and minimize this but just know that's a characteristic of alder. Additional sanding, wood conditioners, glazing and multiple step finishes can all minimize the amount of blotchiness on the alder.

10. Hardwood Flooring – Shrinkage in hardwood flooring is normal due to weather changes and the amount of humidity in your home. We recommend a "V-groove" and/or rustic wood floor design to minimize the visual impact caused by shrinkage. Our floors are covered by a limited warranty. We guarantee the grade of material and workmanship for one year. We guarantee the moisture content at the time of installation is within industry standards. We cannot guarantee against cupping, buckling or shrinkage because of improper care or climate conditions beyond our control. Some cleaners can be harmful to wood floor finishes. Your "Homeowners Manuel" will clarify what products can be used on your wood floor.

11. Wood Doors – Wood doors will shrink over time. This shrinkage can cause warping and changes in the way the door operates. Warping isn't considered a defect unless it exceeds .25" over 7'0" in the plane of the door. It's rare to set a door that will remain completely sealed in all weather conditions due to the amount of shrinkage and movement that will occur in a wood door. Exterior double doors in particular are extremely difficult and our warranty doesn't cover a complete air-tight seal.

12. Shrinkage – Wood products will shrink over time. We will make material recommendations and use installation practices to reduce the possibility of excessive shrinkage during the course of construction. We cannot eliminate shrinkage. Moisture content is a major cause of shrinkage. If your home includes large amounts of wood flooring and timber beams or trusses, then you may want to consider having us add a humidifier to your HVAC system.

13. Euro Style Shower Doors – Euro style shower doors do not seal and will allow water leakage depending on shower design and shower head placement.

14. Lighting Allowance – The lighting allowance includes all lighting fixtures except recessed can lighting unless noted otherwise in the plans or contract documents. Recessed can lights are to be supplied by the electrician.

15. Roof Design and Ice – Complex roof designs often create areas that will ice up, which can lead to ice and water damage. This is weather-related and isn't covered as a warranty item. The use of an Ice & Water Shield, Heat Tape and cold roof systems can help minimize the potential impact from ice and snow.

16. Subcontracts – Subcontract unit pricing and/or time and material bids versus fixed cost bids can both have advantages. Do you prefer fixed cost or time and material? We need exact finishes and details in order for us to get accurate bids.

17. Owner Supplied Material Warranty – We are unable to provide a warranty on owner-supplied materials. Further, late delivery of owner-supplied materials can cause delays and additional costs.

18. Owner Selected Subcontractors – We are unable to take responsibility for warranty, schedule, or the quality of work provided by owner-selected subcontractors. Please include us in planning and scheduling meetings if you choose to select your own subcontractor for a portion of the work. Delays, schedule conflicts and additional costs can occur if you are scheduling work that we aren't aware of and haven't coordinated with other subcontractors. It's also important to understand that there are many ways to build a home and while the subcontractor you select may be capable of excellent work, they may use a different process, that when placed within our system can cause schedule delays and additional costs. We have also found that many times when we work with an owner-selected subcontractor the work is good, but because we haven't worked with them mistakes are made mostly due to poor communication. Occasionally an owner-selected subcontractor works out great and we have a new subcontractor, however it more often causes delays, mistakes, frustration and additional costs.

19. **Warranty** – Upon final completion of the home, a warranty walk through will be scheduled approximately six months later. You should contact us immediately for any major or emergency warranty issues. Any minor things such as tile grout or caulk should be noted and taken care of at the six-month warranty walk through.

20. **Schedule** – We use project scheduling software and do our best to start with a reasonable time schedule. Realize that some slack is built into the schedule and subcontractors don't need to be working at your project every day in order to meet the schedule. There may be times when we're waiting for inspections before work can continue. Excessive weather delays will result in schedule delays. The best thing you can do to help with the schedule is to make your finish decisions early. Remember that most of the items you will be picking are special order and can take several weeks or longer for delivery. During any given project we are faced with four challenges: **Price, Speed, Quality and Service.** Any project can have any three of the four, but it is impossible to have all four. At B&B our goal is to provide the highest possible quality allowed by your budget in a reasonable time. We will not sacrifice quality or price for speed unless specifically requested by an owner and we always want to offer the highest possible service. We will provide you with an owner selection form to track all finish selections. Many finish selections will need to be made and your timely selection of those finishes and completing the owner selection form will directly affect the schedule of your home.

21. **Budgets** – We put a lot of effort into providing an accurate realistic budget that will allow us to complete the project in such a way to meet or exceed your expectations. However, there can be miscommunication and we sometimes make a budget error or miss something. Please review the detailed estimate very closely. If it's not included on the plans and/or isn't specifically listed on the detailed estimate sheet, then it isn't included as part of the budget. To the best of our ability, your budget has been set based on the information you have given us. No matter how high we set budgets it's possible for you to select finishes that will exceed your budget. Additionally, making decisions and designs early allows us to get multiple and more accurate bids and in turn have accurate budgets. Example: Waiting until right before the tiler is about to start to get us tile drawings and selections will really hinder us in getting that budget accurate and can often lead to additional costs above the budget amounts.

22. Contingency – We suggest including a contingency in any project budget. To complete your custom home we will be using thousands of materials together in a way that has never been done before making the project budget an estimate. Contingency funds can be used for items missed or under estimated during the bid process and/or to help cover the cost of increased material and labor costs. In some cases the contingency may also be available to cover the cost of minor change orders.

23. Judgment Calls – During the construction process there will be times when we as your builder will be making some judgment calls. Many of these will be unknown to you, and that's just part of the business. As your builder, we will be making those decisions based on your project budget, schedule and level of quality and as if it was our own home.

24. Change Orders – We suggest setting a limit for verbal change orders. Remember that when requesting work from subcontractors it's important to talk about any potential cost changes. Please do not assume that there will be no increase in the cost. Subcontractors are often anxious to get the work completed and forget to talk about an increased price. We would also suggest that B&B have authority to approve small change orders when within the contingency without your approval.

25. Utilities – Most utility companies will not install any utility lines to the home until the home owner has completed the required forms and often signed contracts. In some cases there will be fees associated with these utility hookups that are not part of the construction estimate. It's often impossible for us to estimate and include these costs as part of your home costs due to the complexity of these utility agreements and contracts with the utility companies.

26. Finalization of Project – We try to have about a month scheduled to allow for punch lists once the project is complete and we have received all of the final inspections. This allows us to do a walk through by ourselves finalizing the finishing touches. Then we try and walk through with the owner and address any other items that are brought up and found. This time really makes a difference in the end quality of your home. We will do everything we can to get you moved in as originally scheduled. If we

try and push and skip over this period, then we'll really have a hard time finalizing all of the little things that we feel set our homes apart.

27. Perfect Project – While we do our very best to offer the highest standards in construction, there is no perfect project and no perfect contractor. Your home will combine thousands of materials in a way that has never been done before, that combined with a unique schedule will create problems and challenges unique to your project. We can offer excellence but not perfection. The term "don't sweat the small stuff," certainly applies to building a custom home. Let us worry about the small stuff; it's what you hired us to do.

Preferred Vendors & Subcontractors

3 Brothers Plumbing

For the past decade co-founders Dominic & Weston Barnes (brothers) have provided Montana with superior plumbing and heating systems. Quality is the foundation upon which Three Brothers Rest. They believe that their customers deserve the highest quality, service, workmanship and material. Located at 3 Albertine Lane, Montana City, Montana, the office can be reached at 406-449-4343 or visit them on the web at 3brothersplumbing.com.

 ## All Phase Construction

For all your drywall, plastering, and EIFS needs. Where quality and service isn't just a promise it is our word. For more information contact All Phase Construction, 2158 Westcliff Drive, Idaho Falls, Idaho or Call Johnny Aguinaga at 208-339-3650, e-mail johnnyaguinaga@cableone.net or Phillip Forbord at 208-604-0670, e-mail pnforbord@cableone.com.

Architectural Elements & Design has many years of design and sourcing experience. They represent the finest lines and sources with expert craftsmen and fabricators. As their name indicates, they provide many elements of architecture for their projects. These include cabinetry, windows, doors, hardware, custom iron and copper and flooring. They have been a valuable partner in many of the finest homes in the Jackson, Wyoming and Big Sky, Montana areas and Southastern Idaho. These include numerous projects in the Yellowstone Club, Granite Ridge, Crescent H, 3-Creeks, Teton Pines, Amangani, Wilderness Ranch, and more. Please contact them at 1705 High School Road, Building 100, Suite 150, Jackson, Wyoming or call 307-732-1020. Also Jane at 307-413-1403 or Doug at 208-251-7433.

B&W Excavating has 17 years of experience in demolition, septic and underground utilities (driveways to highways). They also prepare landscapes which includes rock work, retention walls and pond/water features. Contact Bart Weekes at 208-313-6197 or e-mail him at bart@bwexcavating.com.

 Bryan Landon, owner of **Bryan Landon** Construction, Inc., has been in the concrete industry for 15 years. Located in Eastern Idaho, Bryan Landon Construction, Inc., has been providing premium concrete services on commercial, industrial and residential projects throughout Idaho, Wyoming, Utah and Montana since 2002. They specialize in all aspects of concrete and are able to pour walls of any height and width. Slabs can be stained, polished or stamped to meet any of your aesthetic or structural needs. Their state-of-the-art equipment and expertly trained employees allow them the ability to complete jobs in an efficient and precise manner. Please browse their website at bryanlandonconstruction.com to see pictures of their work, and view our references. You may call them at 208-521-4483 for estimates or any questions that you may have.

Classic Interiors Stainmaster Flooring Center of Idaho Falls has over 25 years of experience in the design and flooring industry and is owned by Mike Peterson. Mike has assembled the finest team of design and flooring professionals in the area. With over 90 years combined experience and hundreds of award winning homes they are anxious to share their knowledge and personalized service that will make your home unique and inviting. They are the regions exclusive source for the Ultralife Stainmaster carpet brands such as Tuftex, Camelot, Royalty and Masland. They also showcase beautiful hardwood, tile and stone from all over the world. Classic Interiors, Inc. is located at 125 South Holmes Avenue in Idaho Falls. Contact them at 208-524-8200 or visit their web site at Classicinteriorsidaho.com.

ColorWorks Painting LLC has over 30 years of experience and has provided quality products and custom paint jobs for its clients in the state of Idaho. The knowledgeable staff can assist you in picking the right product and color for your job. Using current techniques like glazing, staining, and faux finishing, ColorWorks Painting is sure to make a beautiful addition to any home or building. ColorWorks Painting can be contacted at 208-709-4997 or by email at Colorwks@cableone.net .

Custom Designs Inc. Tile and Stone Owned and operated by Travis and Tonya Rogers. They have been doing business for many years and specialize in high end luxurious custom homes including glass and handmade tiles. Their team can assure you the quality and perfection your home deserves.

Their high-end custom work can be viewed on their web site at customtiledesign.net. They can be reached at 406-993-2288, cell 406-640-0388, or email tltintm@hotmail.com.

Devine Design is known for their quality and customer satisfaction. A small team of painters and decorators with over 40 years experience in the industry. They offer an in- house interior decorator and a faux finishing artist trained in the arts in England. Their work has been featured in home shows for the past five years and in many homes and businesses in Southeast Idaho. Tamara Wulf or David Montgomery can be reached at 208-524-7050 or email at montysss@hotmail.com

Layne Hanson has been installing brick, natural stone, and artificial stone since 1983 throughout Southeastern Idaho. He takes great pride in his work and ensures quality on every project by personally working on each and every one. He can be contacted at 208-523-5569, unless he is gone skiing.

Hertz Contracting is a diversified construction company. They have specialized in excavation and have been working on custom homes for years. They take pride in their work and know that the work they do is vital to the entire home. Their work is also the underlayment of the driveway up to the home and the backbone to modern conveniences such as septic, water, electricity, phone, and other under ground utilities. They also play a role in the yard and general appearance of the outdoors. They have offered many other services over the years and are now also offering realtor services. Hertz Contracting is located in Driggs, Idaho, at 208-354-3309 or tetonvalley4sale.com or land@silverstar.com

Home Lighting Center Lighting is the most effective way to transform a room. At **Home Lighting Center** they carry top brands like Murray Feiss, Casablanca and unique one-of-a-kind lighting products you won't find anywhere else. From relaxing and romantic to energizing and inspirational, their expert staff will help you create the right look for any room in your home. They are open daily at 650 West Sunnyside Road. Contact them at 208-523-2300. "Home Lighting Center - Quality you deserve at prices to fit any budget".

J & S Siding Company was started in 1977 by Joe and Stephanie Walrath. Their goal has always been quality, integrity and honesty when working with customers. Their motto is "We take pride in your home". They have completed siding and gutter work from Boise, Idaho to Star Valley, Wyoming and all parts in between. They specialize in Seamless steel siding, including seamless log, but have installed everything from vinyl to fiber cement, to cedar. They pride themselves on their metal trim work and also their seamless gutters. Please contact Joe and Stephanie at 208-522-6624.

Johnson Brothers was founded in 1905 and remains family owned and operated. Their planing mill is one the most progressive woodworking and casework facilities in the Intermountain West. Over the years the business has expanded to include a retail/wholesale store selling quality building supplies throughout southern Idaho and Wyoming. Johnson Brothers' focus remains on craftsmanship, attention to detail, quality standards and exceptional service to meet the needs of customers. Integrity, honesty, dependability, respect for customers and competitors and the quest for excellence are daily goals for the employees at Johnson Brothers. Visit their showrooms at 223 Basalt in Idaho Falls 208-523-8600 or 2240 South Cole Road 208-658-2375 in Boise or on the web at jbros.com.

LC Insulation and Supply is a diverse company whose employees have a real can do attitude. Owned and operated by Lorin and Connie Croft since 2000, this is a total, whole house insulation and weatherization company that serves Southeast Idaho and parts of Montana and Wyoming. Lorin has been in the insulation field since 1983 and his staff has over 53 years of combined insulation experience. They are a great company to do business with and are very customer service oriented. Not only do they specialize in insulation but are also authorized dealers for Sunsetter Awnings, Weathershield windows, and AluminArt storm doors. In 2008, they added a new addition to their many services and are an authorized dealer and installer of SkyStream 3.7 residential wind turbines. Join them at their office and showroom at 606 N. State Street in Shelley, Idaho or they may be reached at 208-357-3939. You may also visit their website which is lcinsul.com. You'll be glad you did.

Liberty Plumbing LLC is owned and operated by Jason and Jennifer Wistisen. They have over 10 years experience in the plumbing trade doing residential and commercial new construction, remodel, service, and restoration. They take pride in their quality workmanship and integrity on every job. Their goal is to make sure their customers are 100% satisfied with their project. Liberty Plumbing is located at 334 North Groveland Road in Blackfoot, Idaho and can be reached at 208-604-5441 or at Libertyplumbingllc@yahoo.com.

 Mathews Plumbing has been serving Southeastern Idaho since 1949. They specialize in residential new construction, but regularly works in all areas from service work to commercial/industrial plumbing. Please visit them at 342 South State Street in Shelley, Idaho or online at mathewsplumbing.net. Contact Gavin Mathews at 208-357-3439 or 208-589-8934.

Metro Tile Metro Tile has been mountain west's premiere residential and commercial tile installation company *Salt Lake City, Utah* for over 35 years. They pride themselves in their exceptional quality of work and customer service. Please visit them at www.metrotileutah.com to view their company history and experience their showroom. Doug Davenport is available at 801-433-0168.

Merrill Woodworking & Design is located in Rigby, Idaho. They have over 34 years of experience in the cabinetry and woodworking business and provide cabinet and custom wood furniture services for both commercial and residential needs. Their shop at Merrill Woodworking & Design has state-of-the-art computerized machinery which ensures accuracy and quality for the finished product. They have unlimited selections of stains, glazes, toners, colors, and wood types to accommodate any style of cabinetry you may desire. At Merrill Woodworking they pride themselves on providing top quality products suitable for every budget and lifestyle and spend quality time giving attention to fine detail on each and every job. They look forward to serving you and all of your fine cabinetry needs at 659 North 4128 East, Rigby, Idaho. Contact Kent at 208-745-7320 or 208-390-6328 or Merrillwoodworking.com.

Peak Flooring of Idaho, Inc. is owned by Keith and Melissa Cain. They pride themselves in quality second-to-none. They are a full service wood flooring business that specializes in installing, sanding and finishing <u>new</u> and refinishing your <u>existing</u> wood floors. If you need a stairway installed or have a custom border in mind, they can take care of it for you. Located at 152 E. Main, Suite 104, Rigby, Idaho. Contact Keith at 208-317-7325 or 208-745-7325, Peakwoodfloors@hotmail.com.

Petersen & Associates Inc. is a family owned Masonry business centered in Jackson, Wyoming. They offer high quality custom rock installation, as well as commercial and decorative block work across all of Western Wyoming and Southeast Idaho. Please contact them with your stone needs at 307-733-4191 or e-mail at Petersen1@qwestoffice.net.

Precision Tile is your best source for quality and innovation when looking to install natural stone, mosaics, ceramic and porcelain tiles. They bring a vast range of knowledge and experience to the table when helping you design and install your custom tile work with prices that can't be beat and a satisfaction guarantee. Contact them at 208-681-0087 or by e-mail ryanwdhs@yahoo.com.

Pure Water Plus is owned by Bruce Ottley a custom water conditioning company located in Rigby, Idaho. The company has been serving all of Southeastern Idaho and surrounding communities since 1999 as an authorized representative of The Reionator System provided by Water Tech Industries; a well-established company that has been solving water treatment issues since 1987. Bruce was honored as the number one salesman in 2004 and has been listed among the top ten dealers of Water Tech for both sales & service the past six years running. He knows water and would like to show you how to See, Feel, & Taste a difference in your water today. Visit their website at Purewaterplus.biz or call Bruce at 208-317-7700.

RoofTop Solutions, Inc. is an excellent roofing company owned by Jason and Cara Briggs, established in Rigby, Idaho. Jason has over 15 years experience in a variety of roofing applications, such as; single-ply, shingles, shakes, metal, and copper, along with many other specialty materials. RTS has professional roofing crews here to serve all of your roofing needs. Call them at 208-745-6860 or visit them on the web at rooftopsolutions.biz.

Simkins Hallin is the largest and most capable single-location building material supplier in the region. Their volume and direct buying power means considerable savings are passed on to their customers. Their free-delivery range stretches out hundreds of mile sin each direction. Working remotely with internet account access and cell phones, Simkins Hallin can bring tremendous efficiences to your job. If you're in the market for a framing package, trusses, roofing, siding, doors, windows, cabinets or other building materials, call 800-823-8733 or e-mail us at simkins-hallin.com.

 You can put your trust in **Solid Stone Inc.** They provide the best quality products at wholesale prices. Their unparalleled service, competitive prices and overall value are why loyal customers won't go anywhere else. They look forward to serving you! Solid Stone Inc. is a name you can trust. Contact Colin Holm at 208-521-3674 for more information or visit us on the web at solidstoneinc.com. To see our online gallery go to solidstoneinc.blogspot.com

Sommers Plastering Company is owned by Cary Nielson who has over 30 years of experience in old traditional interior lath and plaster along with the new veneers and colored finishes. They also apply 3 coat stucco systems with various finishes. Contact them at 208-523-9542.

 Squires Brick, Inc. is a locally owned family business that has supplied the masonry needs of eastern Idaho for over 38 years. They help their clients select from brick and stone veneers, as well as decorative pavers and wall systems for landscaping. They pride themselves in customer service and product support. You can contact them in Rexburg at (208) 356-3324, in Idaho Falls at 208-523-7955, or email them at Squiresif@ida.net.

 Stoneworks Custom Granite & Marble, LLC has been bringing homeowners custom granite work since 1998. Being locally owned and operated lets us provide good old fashioned customer service, while using the best materials and cutting edge technology to fabricate your project. Stoneworks specializes in natural stone products for all applications, including residential and

commercial. Visit them at 12499 West Reservation Road, Pocatello, Idaho, or at stoneworkscustom.com. Call them at 208-237-0696.

Taylor'd Electric, LLC specializes in high-end, custom, residential homes, as well as commercial and industrial wiring. Owner, Jared Taylor, has over thirteen years experience and has worked with B&B Builders for the past five. Taylor honors honesty and integrity first in working with his employees and customers. His homes have been celebrated in three different "Parade of Home" shows and have won multiple awards. Taylor'd Electric has the highest quality of work with the highest standard in employees. You may contact Taylor'd Electric at 208-604-2529 or email them at taylordelectric@gmail.com.

 **West Pointe Electric Inc.** was established by Thomas Causey and Steve Schultz with a vision to provide the client with a project of unsurpassed quality, delivered in a timely manner, for the most economic value. In order to accomplish our mission, West Pointe Electric, Inc. commits, without reservation, to learn and understand each and every client's needs as they relate to timing, quality and cost. Thomas Causey and Steve Schultz, with a combined 28 years of electrical and management experience, formed West Pointe Electric in April 2005 and shortly thereafter hired Travis Foley as the company's Senior Estimator. Travis brings over 20 years of electrical estimating and management experience to the West Pointe Electric team. The company has since experienced extraordinary growth successfully completing over 150 residential projects ranging from $ 15,000 to well over $ 300,000 in areas such as Jackson Hole Wyoming, Teton Valley Idaho, Idaho Falls Idaho, Star Valley Wyoming and Rexburg Idaho. Over the same period of time, West Pointe Electric Inc. also has completed multiple commercial projects including banking institutions, restaurants, governmental facilities, retail office space and The Teton Springs Marketing Center. In addition, West Pointe Electric has a full time service department meeting the electrical needs of clients in Southeastern Idaho and Wyoming. West Pointe Electric, Inc. has established itself as an industry leader in the region providing each client with a detailed personalized and realistic plan to ensure uncompromised quality and unparalleled personal service. Contact them at 208-354-0400 or wpe@tetontel.com .

About B&B Builders, Inc.

B&B has been building beautiful custom homes and commercial properties since its inception in 1993. Today the family-owned business builds some of the most desirable luxury custom home estates in Southeast Idaho.

B&B has participated annually in the Parade of Homes since 1997 and has won numerous awards year after year for creative design and quality construction. They are members of the Homebuilders Association and the National Federation of Independent Businesses, the nation's leading advocate for small and independent business owners around the country.

B&B Builders strives every day to meet the needs of their clients. Ben and Brent meet with each homeowner at the beginning of the planning process and design a budget that works around the homeowner's goals, needs and lifestyle. Weekly meetings at the job sites and email communication keep the homeowner, project manager and other team leaders focused on the key steps of construction. Utilizing a network of the most talented architects and skilled subcontractors in the area, B&B is able to offer a one-stop approach to completely design, build and furnish a luxury home. Clients don't have to limit their choices on fixtures to just a few select items–they can customize every furnishing down to the last detail. Homeowners know when they come to B&B Builders that their home will be built the way they want it done.

Ben and Brent Johnson set out to build a company the way they thought it should be done and how they'd like to be treated if it was their own home under construction. Integrity, quality, service and communication are the building blocks behind B&B Builders' sterling reputation in the home construction community.

B&B recognizes that although building beautiful homes is what they do every day, it's important to remember that for each one of their homeowners it's the only home that matters.

Visit www.bbbuilders.com for more information

ABOUT THE AUTHORS
Ben A. & Brent L. Johnson
Owners
B&B Builders, Inc.
—❦—

 As young children, Ben and Brent Johnson saw their share of home construction projects first hand while working for their father's ornamental iron business. A strong business philosophy helped foster the brothers' interest in home construction and led them to founding B&B Builders in 1993. Today, the family-owned business builds high-end residential custom homes in eastern Idaho, Wyoming, Montana and Utah.

Ben received a degree in industrial technology while Brent graduated with a master's degree in accounting. Ben and his wife, Lauri, have three sons and Brent and his wife, Jenny, have two sons and two daughters. Both live and raise their families in the Rigby, Idaho area. This is their first book.

Dave Konkol
President
Dave Konkol Homes, Inc.
—❦—

Dave Konkol has been creating some of the most beautiful and well designed homes in Florida for more than 20 years. He is the founder and president of Dave Konkol Homes, Inc., a custom home building company specializing in luxury homes. He graduated from the University of Wisconsin-Stout with a degree in Construction Management. Dave is a civic leader, sports enthusiast, and marathon runner.

NOTES

NOTES

NOTES

NOTES

NOTES

NOTES